Praise for *Ron Kardashian's 30-Second Solution*

"It is my firm belief that it's impossible to make good decisions without good information. *Ron Kardashian's 30-Second Solution* introduces readers to new breakthrough information for transforming old patterns into dramatic turnarounds for those who want to derive purpose and more satisfaction from life."

—**Bishop T. D. Jakes**, *New York Times* bestselling author, *Reposition Yourself: Living a Life Without Limits*

"The game of life is measured in seconds. The quality of your life, your health, your relationships, your finances may be the result of years of behavior, but each course was set in seconds. If you're looking to transform every aspect of yourself to the very core, I recommend you read and implement *Ron Kardashian's 30-Second Solution*. Get ready: Your life is about to change."

—**Jordan Rubin**, *New York Times* bestselling author of *The Maker's Diet*

"Ron Kardashian is brilliant! His amazing book is going to help you change and see results in your life! As a clinical psychologist, I work with people every day to help them take action that will give them the desired results. *Ron Kardashian's 30-Second Solution* gives insights and tools to achieve lasting success."

—**Michelle Golland, Psy.D.**

RON KARDASHIAN'S
30
SECOND
SOLUTION

TRANSFORM YOUR BODY, BUSINESS, RELATIONSHIPS, AND LIFE IN JUST SECONDS AT A TIME

FOREWORD BY
DANIEL AMEN, M.D.

Health Communications, Inc.
Deerfield Beach, Florida

www.hcibooks.com

Library of Congress Cataloging-in-Publication Data

Kardashian, Ron.
  Ron Kardashian's 30-second solution : transform your body, business,
relationships, and life in seconds at a time / Ron Kardashian.
    p. cm.
  Includes index.
  ISBN-13: 978-0-7573-1585-5 (trade paper)
  ISBN-10: 0-7573-1585-2 (trade paper)
  ISBN-13: 978-0-7573-9163-7 (e-book)
  ISBN-10: 0-7573-9163-X (e-book)
  1. Thought and thinking. 2. Mind and body. 3. Positive
psychology. 4. Success. 5. Success in business. I. Title.
II. Title: 30 second solution. III. Title: Thirty-second solution.
BF441.K259 2011
158--dc23

                                                    2011026159

©2011 Ron Kardashian

Publisher: Health Communications, Inc.
          3201 S.W. 15th Street
          Deerfield Beach, FL 33442–8190

Cover design by Justin Rotkowitz
Interior design and formatting by Dawn Von Strolley Grove

This book is dedicated to YOU, the reader.
Life is a process that will lead you to your promised land.
Grow comfortable with that process
and the process written within these pages:
They work! Go for your dreams!
Never give up, and you will see all
your desires come to pass! I'm with you!

CONTENTS

FOREWORD

I write the forewords to very few books. I decided to do this one because this topic is so important and Ron delivers his message in a way that is easy to understand and apply. Forethought and focus are two of the most important ingredients of success in any endeavor you undertake from relationships to health to money—everything.

If you put into practice *Ron Kardashian's 30-Second Solution* it will help you develop new brain pathways that will enhance impulse control, focus, and forethought.

Your brain is involved in everything you do, including how you think, how you feel, how you act, and every decision you make. When your brain works right, you work right. When your brain is troubled, you are much more likely to have trouble in your life. I often say that your brain is like a computer that has both hardware and software. Optimizing the physical functioning of the brain increases your chances for success in all you do. This means avoiding things that hurt the brain such as brain injuries, drug and alcohol abuse, poor diet, insomnia, lack of exercise, smoking, and negative thinking patterns; and engaging in regular brain-healthy habits such as exercise, great nutrition, ingesting omega-3 fatty acids, new learning, and getting good, consistent sleep.

Once you optimize the physical functioning of the brain, it has to be properly programmed for you to get the most from it. Impulse control, focus, and forethought are indeed all brain functions, but your day-to-day behavior can enhance these skills and your success, or they can diminish these skills and limit your success. Your behavior is shaping your brain in positive and negative ways.

Ron Kardashian's 30-Second Solution will help you put a brake on the brain to help you think before you act so you make significantly better decisions. It gives you a powerful mechanism to engage the most human, thoughtful part of the brain known as the prefrontal cortex.

The prefrontal cortex is the front third of the brain; and it is considered the brain's executive center because, like the boss at work, it is associated with forethought, judgment, impulse control, organization, planning, focus, empathy, and learning from mistakes. When the prefrontal cortex works right, people follow through on their goals despite challenges and obstacles. When the prefrontal cortex is hurt or low in function, for whatever reason, such as having ADHD or sustaining a brain injury, these functions become compromised. When the prefrontal cortex works too hard, people tend to get stuck in negative thoughts or negative behaviors.

The exciting news, something that has motivated my life for the last twenty years, is that you can change your brain and change your life. You can literally enhance the actual physical functioning of the brain, including the prefrontal cortex. By reading *Ron Kardashian's 30-Second Solution* carefully and practicing the exercises in it, I am confident you will enhance your prefrontal cortex and develop better patterns that will enhance your life.

Congratulations, you are about to embark on a very important journey to a better brain and a better life. It literally can take 30 seconds to ruin your life with bad decisions, as you will see, but it can also take a very short period of time to help you keep on track.

To your brain health,
Daniel G. Amen, M.D.
New York Times bestselling author of
Change Your Brain, Change Your Body

Acknowledgments

Thank you, my gorgeous wife. I am forever grateful for the abundance of grace you have allotted me in helping me not only to write my book, but also to help me rewrite the chapters of my personal life. Your love and support over the years is a testimony to the power of unconditional love. True love is possible, attainable, and life altering. You have been the ultimate coach, not only through your words, but also through the strength of remaining patient and kind. *Humility* and *honor* are two words I never thought I would use together, yet when I hold you in my arms and look in your eyes, it's these two words that fill my heart. This book could never have been written without the brilliance of you as my wife and lifelong best friend. I'm the wealthiest man alive because of the woman you are! I love you and I thank you!

My children are my heritage, my greatest investment, and

legacy. The art of becoming a father has taken the very best out of me and helped me to understand those around me. You have taught me so much, and I will always be thankful for you and I will always stand with you. You will prosper and increase more and more every year. Let excellence, kindness, honor, and love be our cornerstone forever. Both of you are the living heritage of a future generation that will achieve great things. Never give up, my little angels. I believe in you and will never fail you! Now, let's get some ice cream.

Behind every great coach, there is a greater coach! To all my mentors, coaches, and friends: you have forever marked me with an indelible thought that can never be erased, and that is, "Big business and big money will always come; keep your integrity, your marriage and your fatherhood just as big!" Your coaching over the years has polished the writings of my literature. I will forever be grateful for our relationship and the adoration you have shown to me and my family.

Finally, I acknowledge the warfare that has surrounded my life! Why? It's only through resistance training that we increase the lean muscle tissue. Every setback has been a set *up* to either "give up" or "go up" to another level of strength, power, and development. It's through the struggle that we gain the interior fortitude to get stronger and achieve higher. For me, the haters have been my helpers, The pain has been a platform, and a fight that has led to the wonderful life I'm living today. The saying is true: "For opposition surrounds the birth of many miracles." I'm living proof.

INTRODUCTION: SMALL CHANGES, BIG RESULTS

Have you ever asked a friend, a counselor, pastor, or even your doctor any of these questions:

"How do I lose these last pounds?"

"How do I ask for a promotion?"

"How do I find the man of my dreams?"

"How do I stop thinking negative thoughts?"

"How do I start my own business?"

"How do I take my company to the next level?"

"How do I get my life back on track?"

If so, you're just like millions of people who are struggling to make important changes. Why are so many good, well-intentioned people unable to achieve their goals and enjoy the lives they desire?

As a professional corporate CEO's life coach and fitness expert, I am a *solutionist*, a term I coined for a person who finds solutions to major dilemmas and problems. I help the strongest of headstrong individuals break through their issues and achieve success in business, relationships, finance, and fitness. I am going to share with you a proven method for retraining your brain to think, speak, and act in ways that troubleshoot problems and create solutions for you.

Let's face it, in a very short time, the world has changed exponentially. We are more connected than ever before, typing texts and Tweets in rapid-fire; however, many of us are so "plugged in" to what everyone else is doing that we are disconnected from ourselves and the moment. In a sea of Facebook "friends," many of us lack true connection and a valid support system in times of stress. (Think about it: You would more than likely announce that you had sushi for lunch than you would admit to being home alone, depressed, and eating a pint of Häagen-Dazs.)

What's more, we have access to more information than most of us can process effectively, and we have unlimited choices at our fingertips 24/7, which oftentimes delude us, distract us, and derail us from our goals. Even steadfast people can be felled by our "doom and gloom" society, which sends viral negativity and calamity with just one click of the "send" button. While modern life has changed rapidly, our human brains haven't. This proves problematic when we try to adapt to change, whether it's eating healthier, getting to the gym, or paying off our credit card debt. Today, change requires more than good intentions: lasting change requires a combination of positivity, precision, and purpose!

In this book, I will introduce the 30-Second Solution, a powerful process and perspective shift that will bring positivity, precision, and purpose to your thoughts, words, and actions. It will make the pause button—not the fast-forward switch—your default setting. Most of us live life as if we've ripped the pause button off our own personal remote controls and hit fast-forward instead! People don't think about things, the ramifications, or even the benefits before making a move. The 30-Second Solution will help you install the right brake pads on your brain when you're responding in rapid-fire, and it will help you reset your brain to think positively instead of negatively. The beauty and the simplicity of the 30-Second Solution is that it will teach you how to pause, reflect on, focus on, and troubleshoot problems so that you will create what we are all looking for: solutions and success. As the times are change and intensify, so must we! People are on edge like never before; they are hurting, going through their own issues, involved with dilemmas, and facing circumstances that many of us cannot fathom. As a culture, we need to find thoughtful solutions to these issues and circumstances so that we are part of the solution and not part of the problem. Where could you use more solutions? More specifically, what are the biggest areas of your life in which you need improvement? Money? Health? Business? Relationships? Spirituality?

If you truly embrace the 30-Second Solution,
this book will yield results.

If you embrace the fact that 30 seconds can change your life, it will happen. Have you been under a lot of pressure lately? Are you distressed and even more disoriented than you used to be? This could mean that this is exactly the right moment to move into something new. It is mainly during times of great stress that people move into their times of greatest strength—that is, if they choose to.

You may be struggling from day to day just to make ends meet, be it physically, financially, emotionally, mentally, or spiritually. Or you may be struggling to find meaning in your life. Or perhaps you're like one of the CEOs I've coached who was making more money than he could ask for, yet he felt empty and unfulfilled. Regardless of what you're struggling with at this point, you may feel as though you are merely surviving. Don't get me wrong; surviving is fine—if you're a caveman! The fact is, we live in a world rich with opportunity to grow, learn, manifest our dreams, succeed, and find happiness, security, and contentment. But you can't take advantage of all that opportunity if every second of every day is spent in survival mode. Worry and wonder, worry and fear, fear and torment. Up and down, high and then low. What you need in your life is less survival and more revival!

While some of the decisions you make in your life may take a lifetime to live out, you need to learn how to make the right decisions in the first place. That's what I'll be teaching you in this book, by changing how you think, speak, and act. By introducing new cognitive behavior patterns, you'll learn how to change your thinking, which will then change your feelings and, ultimately, your actions. And yes, it is possible to do this in 30 seconds. When it comes to making the big decisions, we can't overlook the smaller ones. In fact, just as millions of little dots make up what you see in a photograph or a picture, so do millions of daily, seemingly insignificant decisions create the reality that is your current life. Think of this as a deposit and withdrawal system. If you deposit small amounts into a bank multiple times per day, at the end of the week you're going to have a considerable amount. If you continue to take, take, take money out all the time, there will be nothing left. The 30-Second Solution is a deposit/withdrawal system. Each day we have a choice to make quality deposits in our life or make poor decisions that in essence withdraw the resources out of us—resources we should be keeping within ourselves.

If you're overweight, do you think that you became that way overnight, with one simple decision? If you're in a job that you hate, did you just start it? Or have you been there for years, maybe even decades? If you're broke today, is it because you went out and spent hundreds of thousands of dollars last night? Or is it because every day you spent a little more than you should?

The fact is that every bite we put into our mouths is an opportunity to lose or gain weight. Every second we move—or don't move—is an opportunity to feel and look better, or not. Every time we open our mouths gives us the opportunity to say the right thing or the wrong thing. Take it from me: 30 seconds is all you need to have a dramatic turnaround. Seconds do matter! Ask a man or woman who is having a massive heart attack and needs medical attention—30 seconds is critical. I want you to get out of your old mind-set right now and kill the thought process that this book is just another gimmick. Did you know that you could live without food for months, water for days, but you can only live without oxygen for a few seconds? Shift that concept into your behavior patterns. In seconds you could make or break yourself. I have seen people speak haphazardly and completely ruin their careers. Or perhaps you have seen a court trial and the one person says something in seconds that completely ruins his life. Your ability to change—most certainly—can begin right now. And whoever said seconds don't count? You better take a second and laugh at that, because it's simply not true.

I teach people all over the world, and I will show you, too, how to undergo a perspective shift. That is what great coaches do: they challenge you to do better than you would ever expect or do yourself and they let you see things in a different way. Consider me your executive life coach. Let me use this picture to illustrate how powerful a perspective can be: your eye is looking at this picture, but so am I, and most likely what I see is not what you see—until I give you a new perspective. Okay, ready? Turn to the next page and look at the illustration. What do you see?

Initially you saw a toad, but I saw the thoroughbred horse. Now turn the book slowly counterclockwise. What do you see now? When I had you look at it from a different angle, you could see the thoroughbred too. In the same way, you may see yourself as a toad, but with a simple change in perspective you will be able to see yourself as I see you—as a thoroughbred! How you see yourself will determine what your brain thinks, how you feel, and ultimately how you act. Will you hop like a toad or gallop like a thoroughbred? Let the coaching process work in you. Let me help you see life from a different angle.

I believe you have greatness within you. You are born with it. But it needs to be trained, looked at from a different perspective, coached, believed in, and encouraged until you can see and live out your full potential on your own. This book will give you another way of looking at yourself, and I guarantee that you will like the result. Strong muscles develop through repetition, and it's the same with your brain. This book will teach you how to flex your brain muscles in more positive ways. You will train your brain and learn new behaviors and habits in the process. I heard someone once say, "Repetition is the mother of mastery." The tools in this book are the basics of life mastery.

The coaching in this book can propel you forward and break your old boundaries. This can work in any area of your life, including, but not limited to, the following:

- Accelerate your life and your company.
- Foster stronger relationships.
- Give you the freedom to work smarter rather than harder.
- Help you acquire more wealth.
- Improve your health and maintain weight loss.
- Give you better communication skills.
- Land the job of your dreams.

Let's get started! But first, let's get real!

CHAPTER 1

My Success Is Your Success

I want you to know that this book is not just a labor of love but also an expression of my sincere and honest love of life development. To me, life is a gift. At times, some of us have to hit "rock bottom" in order to achieve the greatest heights. Unfortunately, one of those people was me. The good news is when you're at the bottom, there is no place to go but up. I have overcome too many adversities not to appreciate life, and I have learned a lot in the process. As a very sick little guy and then later in life losing everything monetarily, my success is now your success! I was on and off medication for serious medical ailments, and I had serious trouble in school. I buried my troubles in food and became very overweight. I was miserable, lost, and broke.

The older I got, the more mixed-up I became. By the time I entered my late teens and early twenties, I was seriously depressed. I cared little whether I lived or died. "Live fast and die young" became my motto, and I chose my friends accordingly. Of course, my new "friends" turned out to be anything but. I was kicked out of my junior-high-school district, thanks to the trouble I'd gotten into with my so-called friends, but that didn't keep me from tagging along in whatever mischief they decided to try next.

To hide the shame about my weight, my grades, and my aimless life, I began using and abusing drugs. As I started high school, I also added alcohol to the mix. I overdosed several times over the years. I was an equal-opportunity abuser; whatever anybody had and was willing to share, I was up for. Substance abuse nearly killed me more than once, and I didn't care. I found it too exhilarating always looking for the next high.

I enjoyed the fast lane, or at least I told myself I did. Losing weight and living dangerously made me popular; no one cared that I was aching inside or barely passing my classes. After high school I wandered aimlessly through a myriad of part-time jobs—and part-time flophouses. I'd make some money, move out of my parents' house, lose the job, move back home, get a new job, move out again, lose the job, and move back home.

I was thinner than ever and physically had it together (so I thought), so I started modeling. The lifestyle gave me power; I was living in a world of make-believe, where designer clothes and sexy women were all part of the job description, which seemed normal to me. You may know I am related to the very famous Kardashian family, but that celebrity status started long before anyone knew of the Kardashians. In the 1960s, my dad had already made it in Hollywood as Michael Ansara's son on a famous TV series called *Wagon Train*. He was running around with stars like Johnny Mathis and Jerry Lewis. Of course, this was before I was born, but the stories he told me never made Hollywood sound very appealing. Yet I was curious, and frankly, the success he achieved at such a young age did intrigue me. As a result, modeling became my Hollywood and gave me the money as well as a lifestyle that other people were attracted to—and even envied. But the lifestyle was killing me, and often I see this with the young celebrities I coach today. I know firsthand that if you're looking for your fifteen minutes of fame and your motives are wrong, it can kill you. If you don't have a purpose, positivity, and a precise way of executing within your actions—the concepts I teach you in this book—you are likely to become a statistic and completely destroy yourself or your dreams. I certainly was not ready at twenty-two and needed a coach myself!

This pattern of living "fast and furious" only accelerated what could have been a very short-lived life—until my so-called friends and I got the better of me again. One night, we were arrested. I faced serious jail time, but fortunately I wound up serving only a few months on a work farm. It should have been my rock bottom, but it wasn't. Upon my release from the work farm, I returned to modeling and life in the fast lane, with girlfriends and money I then lost in bad investments. This time around though, something fundamental had changed: I no longer found it satisfying to live life in the fast lane, and I felt that God wanted more for my life, rather than for me to end it at twenty-two! So I chose to make a change. A change that took a sum total of about 30 seconds that forever shifted my mind-set and caused me to want more of the right things and less of the wrong ones.

You may have breath in your lungs, but that does not mean that you are living.

Ron Kardashian

The choice to STOP and make this 30-second decision to do more of the right things for my body, my mind, and my spirit eventually led me to consult several prominent self-help gurus, coaches, and pastors who helped me realize that there was more to life than skin-deep beauty; that true beauty could only be found when the body, mind, and spirit worked together. I began to embrace fitness and nutrition to heal my ailing body from the inside out. I stopped my relationship with drugs, including prescription drugs. I prayed a very simple 30-second prayer and began eating healthier, exercising my body and mind, and making an effort to love others in the right way. The lights were beginning to come on inside my soul and spirit.

My mentors helped me see my true talent: I was an encourager, someone who could spot the best in others and lead them to their own true fulfillment. I had always been a nurturer and a high-intensity coach at heart. Part of the reason I always fell in with the wrong group of friends was that it was easier to try to fix their problems than it was to face my own.

I began taking classes in human performance, business coaching, personal development, and theology. I was eager to get my certification and degree in all of them so that I could put my nurturing and encouraging nature to good use.

In 1994, my personal goal was finally achieved: I became CEO of a successful life-balance company. For the past fifteen years, I have inspired multitudes of people all over the world to reach their full physical, financial, emotional, mental, and spiritual potential.

With more than 12,000 hours of one-on-one coaching under my belt, I have received two consecutive nominations for Personal Trainer of the Year and have been an honored speaker for the National Strength and Conditioning Association, one of the largest institutions on health and fitness in the United States. In short, my addiction to living in the fast lane turned into a ride straight to the top of my field. Today I am honored to share the stage with some of America's top advisors. I restored my portfolios a hundredfold and am living the life of my dreams. What's more, I'm dreaming more and growing every day. I wish I could say that I have arrived, but I believe the day we say that, we're in trouble, because we will always have more to learn. I want to stay as physically fit and as mentally young as I can. And I have found a way to do that, which I'm going to share with you. When we continue to challenge ourselves mentally, we keep our brains in shape, just as exercise keeps us in good physical shape.

I've gained a lot of insight, but I still remember my pain and struggles, and I know, understand, and respect yours. I have been there, and I have battled my way back. Whether you struggle with loneliness, emptiness, attitude problems, or drug or alcohol abuse, or you want better friends, a better-paying job, the right mate, or to look great and optimize your health—I have the solution!

I have been candid about the mistakes I've made in my life for a reason. I believe that when we learn from another person's mistakes, we receive the golden secret to success and wisdom beyond our years. Are you ready for success? Then take a minute and look at five categories in your life where the coaching and growth will begin:

- **Physical:** How do you feel at this moment? Could you get up and walk around the block—or run up a flight of stairs—without panting? Could you help your neighbor move without being laid up for the rest of the week? From the weight rooms to the boardrooms of America, everyone needs great health to optimize great wealth. Optimizing a state of physical momentum in which we move regularly and feel good about it is key to our revival in life.

- **Financial:** Are your finances in order? Are you saddled with debt? Or making so much money that you're spending twice as much? I have found that people who don't respect money don't have a lot of it. Being financially secure doesn't mean the same as being independently wealthy; it means feeling secure with and responsible for how much money comes in—and how much goes out. My very wealthy advisor once said, "Money without purpose makes you comfortable while you are miserable." Money is a defense and a tool; but the highest form of knowledge is not found in the people with the most money, but in the ones who understand and have wisdom about *how* to use money to create the most profitable life for themselves, others, and the world. Realize that it's called "currency" for a reason—it should "flow" into your life and into the lives of others.

• **Emotional:** How do you feel every day? Are you close to an outburst every time something unusual happens? Are you ready to pop at the slightest little thing? Are you faking happiness just to get through the day? Or do you feel joy and contentment throughout the day? Emotional stability is the foundation of financial, professional, and personal success.

• **Mental:** Are you a mental citizen? By that I mean do you participate in intellectual conversations either with others or with yourself? Do you question your own actions and the actions of others? Do you read to develop your mind and vocabulary? Intellectual consideration will make you a valuable employee and a stellar potential leader. For you intellectuals, are you so intellectual you're not humble? It goes both ways. Optimizing your mentality is both fun and smart!

- **Spiritual:** What are you grateful for? Anything? Anyone? To truly understand the power and blessing of life, we have to have an attitude of gratitude. Being grateful for what we have will help us identify and go after what we want to have. Studies show that gratitude increases joy, which is a serotonin booster that promotes good heath, lowers depression, and generates excitement and happiness. Does God play a role in your life? Or does God just sit on the sidelines waiting to be called into your game called "life"? I kept Him there for years! That is, until I prayed a 30-second prayer that forever changed my heart and set my thoughts on a path I could have never dreamed about! I suggest you get my book, *Getting in Shape God's Way*, if you want to get educated on the subject.

Now that you have looked at some areas in your life where growth can begin, it's time to set your goals and commit to your cause, be it physical, financial, emotional, mental, or spiritual.

The grass is greener where you water it. Provide nutrition in the areas you want growth—physically, mentally, financially, or spiritually.

Ron Kardashian

START WITH YOUR CAUSE: WHAT GIVES YOU PURPOSE IN LIFE?

Most people I talk to don't even know what a cause is, let alone have one. Yet it's easy to ascertain. Why are you alive? Are there people, places, or things that you live for? Is your reason for getting out of bed each morning to do something meaningful or to contribute? Or is it something more practical, like paying down the car payment? Unfortunately, most people don't have a cause. They live for the moment, indulging in whatever (or in some cases whoever) feels good, regardless of the consequences to themselves or others.

Your cause could be your children, your spouse, your

parents, a loved one, or a creative passion, a technology, or a world advancement. I believe the reason most people contemplate suicide is that they have lost sight of their cause. I should know; I lived the first half of my life that way! But my whole life changed when I realized there was more to living my life than living for myself. Finding a cause I could care about—helping people live better lives physically, financially, emotionally, mentally, and spiritually—helped galvanize my efforts. A cause gave my life purpose, and I'd (still) be lost without it. My wife, Tia, and I wanted to do more for nonprofits, schools, and the destitute around the globe, so we started a nonprofit organization, the sole cause of which is to increase awareness of health and beautification. We are driven to make the world a better place because we have a cause.

As such, your cause will drive you. People with a cause do more because they are living outside their own heads, doing for others as much as—if not more than—they do for themselves. They have a reason to get up in the morning, a reason to save money, a reason to succeed, a reason to not just live, but thrive. Causes don't have to be political or spiritual, or for that matter even charitable. Examples of causes might include:

- To get a better job
- To explore the creativity of your youth

- To be more attractive to the opposite sex
- To live longer for your children and your partner
- To retire sooner
- To write a book
- To have more money
- To build a company to help the world

When you develop a cause and live for more than yourself, your own pleasure, or the moment, you are moving out of "survival mode" and into "revival mode." Revival mode is a level of living that is spent enjoying a purpose-driven life, and that purpose will propel you.

WHAT ABOUT YOUR PURPOSE?

If there is a problem, there is a solution!

Ron Kardashian

We were all created for a specific purpose, and I believe that our main purpose in life is to be problem solvers. At some point in your life, you are going to be called upon to solve something. So my question for you is: how are you wired? I was the troublemaker in school. I talked in a loud voice, and my friends called me Big Mouth! Turns out, I'm now in the self-help profession. This is how I was "bent," and now I'm an international speaker, speaking on stages in front of audiences from small groups to upwards of tens of thousands of people. Doing television and radio, you have to have a big mouth and, as it turns out, I was perfectly wired for my purpose in life. How are you wired? Who are you at the core of your being?

When you believe in something at the core of your very being, when you have a cause so strong that it becomes the foundation of all you think, speak, and do, it cannot be moved or shaken; thus, the power to fulfill that cause is inevitable. Figuring out how you are bent and what your cause is serve as the first action steps to achieve your cause. This is where we get our uniqueness. I want you to be deliberate in making you the best YOU you can possibly be. And that's why you and your cause are synonymous. Knowing who you are and what your cause is gives you the ability to say, "This is who I am, and if you don't agree with it, that's all right because I've made my peace with it, and no one, not even you, will deter me from my life's mission and the very cause for which I was created."

The economy may change and weaken, but your cause will remain strong!

Ron Kardashian

Why do we need a cause and a purpose? Can't we just go through life consuming and spending and contributing to the problem? No, that's the opposite of why we're here! Know this: every single person reading this book was created for only one thing, and that was to solve a problem. That's why you're here today on planet Earth: you're here as a solution! Believe me, you're not a problem; you're the solution. Your existence is the very sign that our world needs something you have. In order to finish this thing called life, you're going to need a cause and a crystal-clear mission and vision. We will discuss vision toward the end of the book.

According to Daniel Amen, in *Change Your Brain, Change Your Body*, 50 percent of your brain is dedicated to vision. People with no vision are easily misled and often abused. I like to call abuse "abnormal use." These types of people are usually sold on the latest and greatest business idea or product. They jump the gun without thinking it through. I will coach you through this later in the book, but for now I want you to try and begin to clarify what life will look like at the end of your life or how you want it to look years from now. This will save you a lot of money, heartache, and time. That's the beauty of a vision: it's yours! You can envision anything and everything you aspire or desire. And when you do—miracles happen, and they happen in *seconds*! The word *vision* in Hebrew is *hazon*, meaning both "to see" and "coming into being." Thus, vision is your ability to see the end from the beginning. *Webster's Dictionary* states that vision is "the ability to perceive something not actually visible." It's time to envision—to see the end in view. It's somewhat morbid, but sometimes I ask my clients what they would like their obituary to read:

- Loved people
- Was kind-hearted
- Built a company that employed thousands and helped the world

- Gave to charity
- Loved God and honored people
- Respected by his family
- Raised children who excelled and were respected

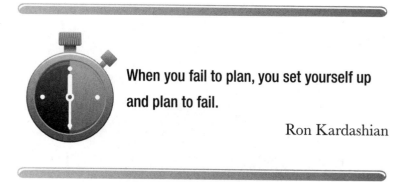

When you fail to plan, you set yourself up and plan to fail.

Ron Kardashian

When you envision your cause, you can set forth an action plan so you will know how to activate your cause, using your purpose and vision to guide you to make it happen. The problem is that very few tap into this amazing power. I have heard experts say that having a mission or vision statement written down is almost like magic. It's not magic; it's a law. You owe it to yourself to have a plan for your life. You may already have a mission or vision, but I am going to challenge you to enlarge it, make it bigger, or fine-tune it. Coaching is an ability to help others become bigger and stronger. Here is a graphic illustration to remind you of how critical your cause is in shaping the values, mission, and vision for your life. It's a visual representation of what I'm going to help you achieve in the last section of the book.

Grab your cause and place it in the center of your life.

Notice that your cause is in the middle. Your cause in life is vital to fulfilling your mission and vision (we will talk more about mission and vision in Chapter 5). If you have not found your cause yet, don't worry—put down what you think it may be. You can use a pencil and then change it later. A cause asks this key question: what are you longing to do in life with all your heart and soul?

In proper order, you must first identify your cause. Identifying your cause will empower you to defy problems that sneak up on you unexpectedly. Remember this phrase: "Identify to defy." Say it over and over again.

So ask yourself, "What do I want to do with my life?" Though your cause may change throughout your life, make some notes here about what you think it might be for this phase of your life now:

_____

_____

_____

Your cause is supported by your values, which is why I have put them at the top. What you value, you will literally die for. In the next chapters, you will learn how to apply the *30-Second Solution* mind-set to how you think, speak, and act to make your cause a reality.

REMEMBER TO FOCUS YOUR VALUE

Your values will give your cause financial, mental, spiritual, and physical adrenaline!

Ron Kardashian

Having a cause is a secret source to fuel your confidence. Coaching everyone from stay-at-home-business moms to corporate giants and pro athletes has shown me that no matter who you are or what you have done, everyone needs confidence and the power to persevere to be a success. Nothing gives you confidence like having your values wrapped around your cause.

Let's focus on what you value. You need this to think right, speak with confidence about your cause, and act with precision. Recognizing what means the most to you in life is vital to seeing your life success in any area. If you don't have values, you will find it very hard to achieve your cause, and for that matter, to fulfill any mission or vision you have. Think of your values as the essence or support beams of your being.

Finally, your values express to the world—and yourself—what you truly hold dear in your life. What do *you* value? What is it that your company values? If you're just starting a company or you aspire to be an entrepreneur, then identifying your values now will solidify your success. Let's take a moment to think of the top values in life. Here are some examples of values from people all over the world:

- Family
- Career
- God
- Making money
- Personal development
- Wife or husband
- Sex
- Organic eating
- Exercise or sports
- Humanitarian service

Do any of these resonate with you?

Now write down your top ten values here. Take a moment and think this through. What do you value?

1. _____

2. _____

3. _____

4. _____

5. _____

6. _____

7. _____

8. _____

9. _____

10. _____

Loving yourself should be a value. If you don't love you, who will? I understand that from time to time we get wonderful, beautiful people in our lives who believe in us more than we believe in ourselves. But when they're not around, you may begin beating yourself up again. You must place value on yourself to validate yourself.

I would suggest you value an interpersonal trait such as conscientiousness or honesty or even character. Of course, when you value these traits, you're more likely to exhibit them and to stick by them when temptation arises.

Whether you are in the process of making lifelong decisions or quick decisions, you must make sure your values line up with your cause. Otherwise, they will just be lip service and not heart service. What I mean by this is that real transformation begins in the mind but sinks twelve inches to your heart where the real power is. Your values should be so deep in your heart that you don't even think about them in your conscious mind.

Whatever you're doing in life, if you do it with "all your heart," you're going to ultimately get greater satisfaction out of whatever it is you're doing. Why do anything in life that you're unhappy about or not completely satisfied with? When you finish this book, you'll see that it has a great ending. You're going to move into a place where you wake up every morning happy, excited, and open to every opportunity that comes with living a wonderful life filled with a cause and a purpose, all supported by what you value most! You can have it, but it is up to you.

Defining moments characterize who you are and what you will become. Now is the time to think about you. Your cause in life, your purpose in life, your passions in life. And not just those things that can make you rich, but the very things that will make you wealthy: physically, mentally, emotionally, spiritually, and then financially. Wealth is a state of being. Think about what brings you the most joy and what you love to do, and go after that with all your heart, mind, and strength.

CHAPTER 2

Think Positively: Harness the Power of Your Thoughts

You could do something in a second
that could make or break a lifetime! Seconds do matter.

Ron Kardashian

Our lives are not made up of the huge decisions, the big breaks, the gigantic opportunities, or the momentous occasions. Our lives are made up of the small, the tiny, and the momentary. Every day we have thousands of opportunities—literally, tens of thousands—to make the right decisions that affect both our immediate and long-term future.

It is estimated that people make up to 35,000 decisions per day, most of them relatively minor,[1] from which way to drive to work to what to eat for lunch, from how early to get up to when to go to bed, but also bigger decisions such as "What on earth am I here for?" and "What am I doing with my life?" Every day our brains think from 35,000 to 60,000 thoughts, and more than 2 million processes are rushing through it at lightning speed. However, if we think the same negative thoughts, over and over, how are we really contributing to our brain power?

The good news is that your brain is not locked into place. Growth can happen at any age, so it's never too early to change—or too late. For this reason "thinking green" is just as important as living green. What I mean is, just as you look to use products that enhance the environment also keep yourself free of contamination by bad thoughts or of contaminating others with your negativity. Even if you consider yourself a negative person, a skeptic, or a lost cause, your brain can change, which means you can change too. In fact, according to an article in *Scientific American* magazine, "Scientists are finding that the adult human brain is far more malleable than they once thought. Your behavior and environment can cause substantial rewiring of your brain or a reorganization of its functions."[2]

Dr. Daniel Amen, psychiatrist and medical director of the Amen Clinic, who wrote this book's foreword, specializes in treating ADHD and other brain disorders. He explains: "The brain can change: This is the headline for mental health in the new millennium! We have seen it work for more than eighteen years. The brain is adaptive and influenced by what we do for it. The opposite is also true; the brain can change in a negative way when we do the wrong things."[3] For this reason, becoming aware of our thought patterns is the most critical thing I can stress within this book. In addition, it's now proven that if you are overweight, your brain is suffering. The results of an Amen Clinic research study, published in *Nature Obesity*, has shown that as your weight goes up, the function of your prefrontal cortex (the most human thoughtful part of the brain) goes down.

WHAT *YOU* THINK ABOUT YOU MATTERS!

Most of us take so much time attending to other people that we often don't take care of ourselves. So take a few seconds right now and tell yourself, "I am the most beautiful me." Or if you'd prefer, say: "I am the most successful me." For some of you, it might be difficult to say. External beauty may be obvious, but true inner beauty and success is a distinction that sets you apart. But guess who must believe it before anyone else can? You!

Right now, you must make the decision to like yourself, which will automatically make you more likable to others. Envelop yourself with kindness of thought and a loving heart toward yourself first and then let it flow out to others. If you don't think you're beautiful or successful, who else will? It's what people think about themselves that brings beauty into their lives and the lives of others. Ultimately, you will reflect who you are. Why not shine with the thought, "I'm beautiful in my own special way, no matter what"? *No matter what!* Nobody can be you, nor can anyone compete with how the Creator made you to be.

One of the central keys in retraining your thought patterns is to make sure you're filling your mind with positive versus negative thoughts. Too often, we start with the negative and never get to the positive. Much like poison can kill your body, bad thinking can kill your mind. Your brain is a muscle; you condition it or it dies. Some of these "mind killers" are statements we might make to ourselves on a regular basis. For example:

- I'm always going to be overweight and unattractive.
- I'm never going to be confident enough to pursue my business goals.
- I'm not smart enough to learn new skills for my job.

- I will never make that type of money.
- I'm not talented enough to fulfill my dream
  of being a singer.
- I'm too old.
- My marriage is over; we'll never get that spark back.
- And on and on.

All of these statements are true *if* you believe they are. That little conjunction *if* is so powerful. It literally means "on the condition that." Try replacing *if* with the definition in a sentence this time: "These statements are all true *on the condition that* I believe they are true." This gives *if* an entirely new meaning, doesn't it?

What I want you to see is that your mind may think certain negative things about your life that in reality are not necessarily true. The key is to keep these negative beliefs out of your mind and heart by continually meditating on positive things throughout the day, over and over again. For example, you may exhibit some of your parents' behaviors as you get older. Why? Because we often inherit thought patterns—both positive and negative—that were formed within our family of origin.

From time to time, Tia and I will look at each other and say, "Oh no! That sounded just like my mother [or my father]!" On other occasions, I will repeat word-for-word something a mentor or my parents said that I want to remember forever. The subconscious mind has an amazing power to store things on autopilot, which is why it is so important that you generate positive thoughts.

This can happen only when you renew your mind with powerful truths about what you want to become in life. This desire originates from the deepest part of your interior self. What you continually think about day after day will determine how you live your life. Often, we ruminate for hours on negative self-talk, which requires so much energy that we then don't have enough time or energy left to pursue the things we truly want to accomplish. Watch out for this. Negative self-talk is what I call an "energy thief."

The fact is you don't have to wait until tomorrow to feel beautiful—or smart, strong, sexy, talented, capable, or whatever—you can feel it today. You just have to believe that you really *are* "the most beautiful [or successful]" you. This is why what we believe creates behavioral changes. You're going to have to get to the root cause of *you*. What makes you unique? What makes you *you*? And if there are some areas where you are not happy with you, well, the good news is *you* can change them! This is part of your cause.

But it all starts with what you believe about yourself. Changing these negative thought processes is easier said than done, I know. Ninety-five percent of my clients have serious, oftentimes crippling insecurity issues. But what I find is that most of these issues are self-created, meaning we truly are our own worst enemies when it comes to self-esteem.

You are the most influential person you are going to meet today. You choose your move.

Ron Kardashian

The key to succeeding is believing not only that replacing your negative beliefs with positive ones will affect your self-esteem (and it will!), but also that you're worthy of it working in your life. You will never lose weight, get that promotion, stay faithful, or become a millionaire if you don't (a) believe you can do it and (b) believe you're worthy of having it!

YOU ARE WHAT YOU THINK!

If you believe you are worthless, ugly, inferior, or any number of other negative personal images, you will continually act out those roles because of your self-perception. The source of this thought life inside you may come from parents, teachers, peers, or your own ideas about yourself, gained, perhaps, from comparing yourself to others. Those beliefs that form your self-image are powerful forces that will drive you to become what you believe.

> You become what you think about.
>
> *Earl Nightingale*

You may try to cover up your inner belief system by compensating with acceptable outward behavior. Yet those powerful (though irrational) beliefs will ultimately govern your life, your decisions, and your emotional, mental, and financial business life, eventually overpowering your physical health in ways that cost you more than you want to pay.

This is something that has been time-tested for thousands of years. Its origin is in an ancient proverb: "As a man thinketh in his heart, so is he" (Proverbs 23:7, KJV). Often we can go through life completely unaware of what we are thinking about on a regular basis. Becoming aware of our thought patterns is the most critical thing I can reiterate throughout this book. This awareness is undoubtedly the key to turning our lives around and creating the lives of our dreams!

We become what we behold.

Marshall McLuhan

While it can be hard to believe, it only takes 30 seconds to change your life. It only takes 30 seconds to change a negative thought into a positive one, and when you practice this on a daily basis, countering your negative thoughts with positive ones, the cumulative effect will be life changing. We really do become what we think about ourselves, so every day, take 30 seconds and fill your mind with the best beliefs you have about yourself. I know this is difficult to do when you have low self-esteem, but doing this exercise every day will transform your thought life. Fill your mind and meditate on true (not false) things; on things that are noble, reputable, authentic, compelling, and gracious; the best, not the worst; the beautiful, not the ugly; things to praise, not things to curse. Here are some examples to get you started:

- "I have a strong sound mind, filled with wisdom and love."
- "I have a generous nature and treat my friends with grace and conscientiousness."

- "I am a success!"
- "My past does not dictate my future."
- "I am compassionate toward others."
- "Nothing is impossible for those who believe."

By practicing this 30-second exercise daily or creating your own meditations, you will begin to develop new ways of thinking. When you change your thinking, your heart is touched, and when your heart is touched, your life and actions will align. One of the most encouraging aspects of this development is the proof that the brain can continue to build new neural pathways even into old age. Scientists and medical researchers are discovering that if we exercise our brains just as we do our bodies, it will literally enhance the part of the brain that calls most of the shots: the prefrontal cortex. The prefrontal cortex is the area in the brain that controls complex cognitive behaviors, such as the ability to discern between good and bad, to see how present actions might affect the future, to make decisions, and to be able to key into proper social behavior. Many researchers believe that functions within the prefrontal cortex are closely tied to our personalities. It is no wonder, then, that replacing our negative thought patterns with positive ones not only has the potential to change how we view ourselves but may also result in a healthier brain and, thus, a more positive self-image. Being able to think before we make decisions could literally save lives.

In a recent study at UCLA, psychiatrist Jeff Schwartz studied the brains of people with obsessive-compulsive disorder. He discovered that when these people were treated with antiobsessive medication, PET scans revealed that the overactive parts of their brains slowed toward normal activity. This was a powerful breakthrough because the research proved medications can help heal dysfunctional parts of the brain. However, the findings were even more powerful and striking for patients who were not treated with medication but received behavioral therapy alone. They showed normalization of the abnormal activity in their brains just by changing their thinking.[4] Start changing your own attitude and behavior today by thinking about whom you could ask to help you change. That change may require the help of a coach, a psychologist, or the like. Just making the decision to ask for help is a sign that you want change. Surfing the Web or talking with a friend is the action behind that thought. So pick up the phone and start calling around. Don't be afraid to ask for help and get the change you want to move in your life. It's your time!

THE BATTLE BETWEEN THE EARS

What is belief but a thought? In fact, beliefs are really just thoughts reinforced over time. We are fat because we believe we're not meant to be thin. We are unfaithful because we believe we're not meant to be loyal or just plain don't believe we can be. We are poor because we believe we're not meant to be rich or just don't have what it takes to acquire wealth.

When did these beliefs start? Often in our childhood, when we were told by coaches, teachers, counselors, and sometimes, sadly, our parents, who maybe weren't listening to what they were spewing: "You're fat! You're lazy! You're stupid! You'll never amount to anything. . . ." Unfortunately, these words get ingrained in our minds as thoughts that become battle cries in our own negative war against our self-worth; a war that, by the way, we engage in on a daily basis—and it all goes on between our ears! You have to be careful of who you let speak into your life (including yourself!). Be cautious of what you listen to; it's molding your beliefs.

Case in point: I had a client whose husband was verbally abusing her. Every three to six months, he would just fly off the handle at her. Psychologically, his words affected her business dealings. I offered words of encouragement in one ear: "You've got what it takes. Here are some business strategies; now go for it! You're the best; you can do this." Yet he was yelling in the other ear, "You're a loser; you're never going to get that kind of money; most new businesses fail!" and so on. I finally discerned her lack of financial growth was tied not to her sales force but to her mental force. I had to level with her and say, "You have got to see a marriage therapist. This is not normal!"

Soon after, her husband hit her. She was shattered spiritually, emotionally, and physically. I wanted this client to be safe. I told her that her husband had to be held accountable, and she needed to get help. She acted on my advice. Despite a shattered spirit, she sought help. Today her husband has admitted his wrongs and is getting therapy. After working through her issues with the therapist, this client made more money in one month than she had for an entire year. Thoughts matter!

Over time, any generic, untargeted, or simply false statements we hear from others become beliefs because we internalize them into our own thought patterns and find ways to reinforce them throughout our lives. Every time we look in the mirror and don't like what we see, those negative comments are reinforced: "You're this; you're that!"

You will always create the environment
around you that you have within you.

Ron Kardashian

Every time we go to the ATM and aren't happy with our checking account balance, those negative thoughts are reinforced: "You're never going to have enough money! You're worthless! You'll never amount to anything. . . ." To stop the cycle of negative beliefs and dangerous thoughts, we have to start believing that we're good, beautiful, smart, and above all, worthy.

Let's imagine you wake up and go to get dressed and find that your favorite pants are, well, a little snug. It's really no surprise. You've been stressed at work and burning the candle at both ends and eating zapped, fried, nuked, and fast food most days of the week; now you're paying the piper. Instead of thinking that you're "fat" or "lazy" or "gross," stop and recycle those negative thoughts into something positive. That's right; be your own spiritual recycling center.

Instead of thinking, *I'm fat,* think, *I'm going to eat one less fast-food meal per day this week! I'm getting in shape! I'm thinner! I'm beautiful!* Or *I'm going for a walk!*

Instead of thinking, *I'm lazy,* think, *I'm going to set my alarm early three mornings this week and walk twice around the neighborhood before getting ready for work.* Thoughts can go either way: right into the mental trash heap where they rot and corrode your body, mind, and soul or into your mental recycling center where they can turn into something magical, new, and positive.

PUT THE BRAKES ON YOUR BRAIN AND YOUR EMOTIONS

In addition to thinking negatively, another mistake that many of us make is to not put a lot of forethought or focus into our decisions. We have somewhat of a Nike mentality: "Just Do It!" We're hungry, so we eat anything. We're thirsty, so we drink anything. We have a bad thought, so we catastrophically ruminate on that one thing until it becomes the very thing we feared would happen

What's missing when we fail in a particular area of our lives is the critical decision-making step. If we are to live with purpose, then we must think and act purposefully instead of just surviving. In our hectic lives, we tend to jump right in and make impulsive decisions before taking 30 seconds to consider the long-term consequences. Nothing in your life will change until the consequences of your behavior become real to you. Thirty seconds is a small investment to make—just half a minute out of the 1,440 minutes in a day—and yet taking that pause could save you years of negative consequences. If you don't believe this, just consider a client of mine who had a triple bypass. He boldly admits, "If I would have just listened to Ron, my coach, I would not have had to have two of these surgeries." It would have only taken him 30 seconds to say no to fried and fatty foods that eventually blocked his artery and sent him to the hospital in an ambulance.

We also have a tendency to let our emotions rule our lives. Don't get me wrong—emotions are very useful in our daily lives. On the one hand, they move us onward, pushing our decisions with passion and leading us to inspiration, drama, enthusiasm, motivation, and a host of other positive sensations. On the other hand, they're very hard to regulate. Seconds after inspiring us, motivating us, or bringing us to new heights of ecstasy, our emotions can become hindrances to our progress and create anxiety, uncertainty, self-doubt, and unnecessary fear.

Know this: when you are guided by emotions, you always have to *feel* right before *doing* right. Instead of choosing a path that's best for everyone, you will have a tendency to choose the path that is most convenient—and centers you. This is because emotions are concerned with protecting their own views and paths instead of taking care of responsibilities.[5]

Instead of silencing your emotions, it's better to learn to temper them. When you feel your emotions taking you on that roller-coaster ride, employ the 30-Second Solution and consciously choose to pause before reacting. Then ask yourself, "Are my emotions driving this decision?" When emotions have you in their grip, you need to think through the moment before it becomes unpleasant—or costly.

Remember that action and *r*eaction are *both* actions. Whether you're in an intense discussion with a colleague, your spouse, a sibling, or a stranger, temperance is vital! If you want to act positively, you have no choice but to remain poised and in control of your thoughts and your words, which will result in positive actions.

The key term when it comes to acting or reacting is *self-control*.

I hate it when my emotions get the best of me and I am left feeling regret after saying or doing something I could have avoided merely by pausing and thinking it through.

To avoid that kind of unnecessary and self-inflicted pain, use this simple script: "Stop right now! I am going to wait until I'm a little calmer and then make an objective decision based on both my best interest and the best interest of the other person and create a resolution of the situation that will make us both happy."

Rather than *re*acting based solely on your emotions, act around them. In situations where relationships are involved, whether business or personal, your complaints about the other person may be legitimate, but the way you respond to them may not be if you are responding to them based on negative emotions alone.

Do something positive to counteract your negative emotions. If you're feeling anxious, angry, irrational, or even unhinged and can't seem to let it go, get someone else's opinion on the matter, seek counsel, or ask an advisor what he or she thinks of your situation. If the situation is a little too personal to share with others, then make your decision, speak it to yourself several times out loud so you can "hear" the outcome, then respond. This way, at least you'll know that you thought things through before responding and that you made a concerted effort to avoid reacting based solely on emotions.

SLOW DOWN—YOU CAN'T HIT REWIND

Controlling our thought processes by taking a 30-second time-out when we find ourselves in stressful situations can prevent us from sometimes dire consequences. In a recent interview on the *Dr. Phil* show, Dr. Phil talked with a woman who had been brutally beaten and then severely burned by her boyfriend who was a detective who had snapped under pressure. A 30-second action of cold, harsh, uncontrollable rage had set this woman up in flames. She lived to tell about it. My eyes filled with tears at the very sight of her. Here is what this precious survivor said: "We must remember to think of the outcome of our actions and control them; if a five-year-old child came up to you and slapped you, would you slap him back? Why not? Because you have the ability to control your actions; you choose to do that. It only takes seconds to control yourself with everyone you meet!"

Her story rings in the ears of every human being who has been subject to domestic violence. Reading this, you and I must not only rethink our actions but remind others of the quick ability we have to control our own. The boyfriend is now doing life in prison, and the woman is maimed for life. She, however, finished her statement with, "He may have taken my beauty, but he will never take my dreams and my joy!"

You possess this power and ability to control yourself. Have you ever been in an argument with your mate or a friend and all of a sudden your boss or perhaps a client calls, and in seconds you're saying, "Oh, hi, everything is wonderful, how are you?" In a matter of seconds, you shift from anger to politeness. Why is this? Because we all have an innate desire to be perceived in a certain way. We value acceptance. It's a powerful action and ability you have—to change your response in just seconds!

Remember Serena Williams? Ranked number one in the tennis world. Four consecutive Grand Slam titles. Fashion designer. Cover girl. Bestselling author. A living legend. And yet, despite more than two decades at the top of her game, it took all of 30 seconds to shatter that very public, very positive image and cast serious doubt on Serena's once untarnished legacy.

After what she felt was a bad call during her 2009 U.S. Open semifinal match, Serena unleashed a profanity-laced, threatening tirade on the line judge, allegedly shouting, "I swear to God, I'm [bleep] taking this ball and I'm shoving it down your [bleep] throat." Not only did the outburst cost Serena a healthy fine and the very public rebuke of fellow legend Martina Navratilova, but also it was aired on national TV and watched countless times on YouTube.com and elsewhere.

As Serena later said of the incident, "I need to make it clear to all young people that I handled myself inappropriately, and it's not the way to act." Since then Serena has worked tirelessly to rebuild her tarnished image, but it's been an uphill battle. Few who have witnessed the tirade will ever forget it, and it now lives in infamy, preserved for all time on the Internet. It could have gone so very, very differently. If instead of a 30-second tirade Serena had stepped back and used 30 seconds to think before she spoke, she would've left a more positive image for others to emulate.

Most of us live life as if we've ripped the pause button off of our own personal remote controls and hit fast-forward instead! Imagine if Serena had availed herself of the 30-Second Solution instead of letting her mouth hit "fast-forward" the incident might never have happened.

You can't go back in time and undo the consequences of a bad decision, but you can buy time now and in the future by beginning to make better decisions today. Never underestimate the power of the moment to affect your life in unimaginable ways.

And don't think I'm picking on Serena; we're all human, we all have our faults, and we've all blown up from time to time. Think about it: How often have we ignored the 30-second pause and flown off, half-cocked, and hurt someone we cared about? How often have we "pulled a Serena" and spoken rashly, acted impulsively, and spent the rest of our lives trying to recover from a split-second decision? We've all made these mistakes, and if we're smart, we learn from them.

I see mistakes as investments we make in our future returns: ourselves. When we learn from our mistakes, we make better decisions in the future. We can't live in a bubble and strive for perfection to the point of never taking any risks, trusting our gut, or making bad decisions. Learn to make a better quality *you*! It's a process.

Have you ever heard a person described as "thick-skinned"? It's true that you have to take some hits in life to harden yourself to adversity. The key is to embrace the adversity—as hard as it is—and let it advance you to another level of emotional maturity rather than compromising to avoid those painful moments. Also, when we make mistakes and admit that we have, we grow in humility, and humility helps us be more compassionate toward others when they make mistakes.

Walt Disney, who suffered several creative and professional setbacks before hitting it big with Mickey Mouse, once famously said, "It is good to have a failure while you're young because it teaches you so much. For one thing, it makes you aware that such a thing can happen to anybody, and once you've lived through the worst, you're never quite as vulnerable afterward."

It's the same principle that's at work in weight training. The heavier the weight you're lifting, the stronger the muscle tissue becomes. This is what happens when you embrace your failures as a means to spiritual growth and emotional strength. Every CEO, manager, employer, owner, and founder: Hear me loud and clear, because you are the poster children for this truth. Never be afraid to show your scars from the battles you have encountered—the ones you have won and the ones you have lost! Sharing your mistakes helps other people learn from them so they can avoid what you have gone through. In essence, regardless of the outcome of our mistakes, when we learn from them and teach others, we're always in a win-win situation.

JIMMY'S STORY

I would like to share a story with you about how letting our emotions control us can have major repercussions in our lives. Jimmy, a client of mine, spent the first thirty years of his life building his wealth. He wanted to provide all the luxury for his family he could, but it was at a price he was not ready to pay. I met Jimmy at a very solemn point in his life. My wife and I drove to his amazing 15,000-square-foot mansion, where we were greeted by vineyards and a three-tier waterfall in a circular driveway. We knocked at the fifteen-foot solid cast-iron door. Jimmy answered.

"Man, Jimmy—this is spectacular!" I said. At the time, the property next door was selling for around $10 million, and in comparison to Jimmy's home, it was a dump! As we toured the house, we saw wall-to-wall antique furnishings from all over the world. The distressed wood floors beneath our feet made it feel like we were in an early-world French villa, and the new furnishings blended modern and classic looks the royal family would have adored!

As my eyes scanned the amazing landscape of interior delicacy, a framed five-by-five-feet picture on the wall hooked my attention. "Is this your beautiful family?" I asked. That's when Jimmy's head dropped. The picture was of a beautiful blond-haired, blue-eyed woman with three children and Jimmy.

"Yes," he confessed, "this was my family." Jimmy went on to say that the first thirty years of his life were all about money, money, money. "I wanted to build my career," he explained. "I was a career man, Ron. Only later in my life, my wife had a breakdown and told me she wanted me. I thought to myself, 'You have had me for the past twenty years; what are you talking about?'"

He continued, "For the first thirty years of my life it was all about me, when it should have been all about me and my wife and kids. My wife and I began having problems, and in a 30-second fit of rage, I threw a glass at her and almost hurt her! Now she is gone, and my kids don't want anything to do with me."

My wife and I were overwhelmed by what he said as we stood in that multimillion-dollar estate with everything one could ever want (at least materially). "All those years, I treated my wife like a bulky water glass when I should have been holding her like a fine-stemmed wineglass."

I looked at my precious wife and considered the countless men I was coaching. Then I thought, *That could have been any of us.* Although he had lived at home, he had been mentally and emotionally unavailable; he was at the office all those years. His final comment to us was, "If I would have only stopped for a moment to hear what she was crying out for instead of throwing that glass at her, she might still be home; we could have worked it out!" Though Jimmy's marriage problems couldn't have been cured in 30 seconds, it was his 30-second action that facilitated his wife separating from him.

Jimmy's 30-second mistake serves as an example of countless people who move via impulse and don't take the time to think before they act. You don't have to end up like Jimmy. He is actively trying to get his wife—and his life—back, but she has moved to another state and is going through therapy over the issue.

Success in life is so much more than how much money you have. Most of the people I coach say that money just makes them comfortable while they're miserable. It just does not need to be that way. In fact, you must make a choice to *never* let it be that way. My wife and I learned a lot that afternoon. Jimmy's comment about his "30-second fit of rage" and its effects inspired, in part, the *30-Second Solution*.

This example illustrates that thinking before we act can be the key to preventing a problem. For example, did you know it's far less expensive to prevent a catastrophe than to find yourself in the midst of one? Knowledge is very powerful when we understand ramifications. Consider these costly and preventable examples:

Standard ambulance ride: $100 to $1,500
Massive heart attack: $500 to $10,000 (ER room visit, testing, and so on)
Heart bypass surgery: $20,000 to $30,000 or more (with complications)

Copays: average $5 to $50 per visit

Early death: immeasurable

While one could argue that the financial consequences for many individuals are minimized by their insurance companies, let's not forget that those costs are eventually paid by everyone else when insurance rates rise. Dr. Peter Lindgren of Stockholm Health Economics says, "The economic impact of heart attacks and strokes in the U.S. alone totals nearly $403 billion in medical care and lost productivity annually."

And what about the emotional consequences? Imagine receiving the news that a dear friend or family member just suffered a heart attack or stroke. Circumstances like these take their toll on the psyche. Mental disorders, including anxiety and depression, affect one in ten working-age adults each year, resulting in a loss of approximately 200 million working days per year.

Let's say you develop type 2 diabetes, a debilitating blood-sugar disorder that affects about 8 percent of the population. Now, close your eyes and imagine giving yourself daily insulin injections, losing your vision, or even losing a limb. How would you feel then? How would your family feel? If you already have it, think how wonderful it would be to conquer it! If you begin to think about restoration, healing, and what kinds of foods will restore your health, things will begin to shift. I have seen this work with one of my clients who had diabetes. After giving her information, she agreed to take action. She began mild exercises every day, eliminated the amount of sugar and processed foods she was eating, and within time, her blood sugar level stabilized to the point where she came off all diabetic medication. The power was a 30-second perspective shift: what you visualize will materialize! However, most people don't believe that. But just because they don't believe it does not mean it does not work or that the principle does not exist. Here's my paraphrase from Habakkuk 2:2–3 in the Bible concordance: "Write your vision down on paper; although it tarries, wait for it. It will come to pass." It's just that simple. What you meditate on, you become. "As a man or a woman thinks, so is he or she."

Think about missing out on your grandchildren because you suffered a massive heart attack fueled by decades of fast food and a sedentary lifestyle. These things happen every day. For many, this reality check finally hits home too late—when they're confined to hospital beds and awaiting bypass surgery—but it doesn't have to be that way.

Your new beliefs can start the moment you read this sentence or hear the early warnings from your doctor. Your life will change when the source of your decision making—your brain—starts communicating with your heart. This is how you convert information into realization and knowledge into wisdom. By becoming passionately involved in a decision and how it affects your purpose, you're more likely to act on it rather than just letting it sit on a shelf.

One of my clients who is now almost eighty tells everyone he meets that if he would have taken my suggestions to reduce his food intake and start exercising just a few days per week, he could have avoided two massive heart attacks! The amount of pain he and his family have endured could have been avoided by taking 30 seconds and asking himself, *If I continue to eat like this, will I live long or die early? I might die, and my kids will be majorly affected. However, if I put the fork down during a few meals, my life span would radically be increased and I could prevent premature death. That would really save not only my life but also should I die unexpectedly from a heart attack save my family and friends from unnecessary suffering.* As you work toward your goals, take 30 seconds to think about your actions and how they can cause powerful consequences.

ELIMINATE YOUR ELASTIC CONSCIENCE

Are you one of those people who suffer from some type of "elastic" disorder? What I mean by this is that you get to a place in your life where you do well for a while, but then, over several weeks, just like elastic, you begin to "stretch" your conscious way of thinking a little more loosely about whatever it is you're trying to achieve. You compromise in areas you know you should not be compromising. It's loose, not tight—like keeping the reins of a horse held tightly so the horse does not get out of control.

For instance, if you've been really good on your diet, and you have an elastic conscience, you'll say, "I've been really good during the day, so I can keep eating ice cream at night; I don't have to stop every night!" Then a once-a-week ice cream splurge becomes a nightly habit. Or let's say you've been working on faithfulness in your marriage, but you're away at a big convention and your elastic conscience thinks, "It's okay if I flirt a little; I'm not hurting anyone." Or maybe you've been diligent about improving your work ethic, but one day you rationalize, "I can be late once in a while; I've been on time all month. What are they going to do, fire me?" That's what I call elastic conscience. Eventually the elastic is going to be stretched too far and something is going to break.

It's a subtle attack, and most people never think anything about it. Suddenly, information begins to flow to your brain and your conscience begins to adopt these new, more lackadaisical attitudes—so much for your diet, being faithful, and being on time; so much for real, lasting change of any kind. And like a rubber band stretching each time it's pulled, your conscience begins to stretch as well. This is the *wrong* kind of stretching.

One bowl of ice cream leads to two, two stretches into three, and *boom*—before you know it, those ten pounds you lost last month come back, plus five more! Meanwhile, a harmless flirtation turns into a hug, then a kiss, and finally, a tryst. And after being late once, why not again? Then a sense of entitlement arises and you're no longer grateful for the job you really once wanted. This is no way to treat an employer. The way you leave something (anything) is the way you go into your next venture or life chapter. Now, you may not have control over every situation in your life, but the ones you can control are the ones you need to execute with dignity and self-respect. You deserve to give your best.

You can feel the effects of an elastic conscience in just about every aspect of your life—from those last twenty pounds you've been meaning to lose for, oh, five years now, to that raise you haven't asked for yet, to the same issues that have been dividing your marriage for years and years.

It's the reason New Year's resolutions don't stick—because we stretch our excuses out longer and longer until, the very next year we're "resolving" to do the same thing we resolved last year and the year before! What's the solution to these elastic thoughts? Simple: the slightest sign of compromise with our elastic conscience needs to be shattered by considering the long-term consequences and how they will ruin our goals or crush our reputation.

Resolve to absolutely, positively achieve your goal and think through your actions—this time, next time, and every time. When you're feeling tempted or weak, stop for 30 seconds and envision the consequences of your actions. When life begins to invade your soul on levels where you find yourself stretching the truth, it's a subtle way for your spirit, soul, and body to tell you that you're beginning to dull your senses and you're giving in to an elastic conscience. Stop! Take 30 seconds and say, "I have got to think this through!"

Elastic conscience rears its ugly head in the business world, too. For example, I know some very prominent executives who set very high standards for their companies and for themselves, but over time they become numb to their own values and then make haphazard or spontaneous decisions that cost them big. This is why I pride myself on the proverb that states: "There is wisdom in a multitude of advisors." Even one extra coach or board member could open up a fresh perspective on your idea or concept and prevent corporate embarrassment or even disaster. I remember coaching a very prominent CEO who was offered eight figures for his company, but he had talked himself into selling for high-nine figures instead in a spur-of-the-moment thought! Try $260 million! When I asked him, "Where did you come up with that number? Do you have a written plan to prove you're worth that much? Do you have projections showing revenue conducive to this selling price? In short, do you have a plan? Have you thought this through?"

He said, "No, no, and no."

My reply was, "So, let me get this straight: you're going to just walk into the chairman's office [whom he had already made an appointment with] and tell him you want $260 million for your company with no plan or proof?" I furthered that statement by saying, "This chairman is not looking for a hotshot with some big technology; he is looking for an astute business man who has an action plan. Do you have a verification of how much your company is worth, how about the return on his investment, year-end profits, expenses? Is the plan written down on paper?" No, no, no, were his answers. I concluded by saying that the chairman wanted to see a written plan. He had nothing! This particular client did have values, but letting his conscience stretch out of his normal values almost made him look like a fool at best and lose the opportunity at worst. Instead of using his values to guide him, he made a rash decision based on emotions in the moment. He said, "Ron, thank you for saving me from such embarrassment. I don't know what I was thinking."

I was shocked by this behavior in two areas: (1) how unprepared we can be at times, and (2) how visible this error was to me yet not to him. His perception of going from eight to nine figures on a whim was a slip in his consciousness. It was like an elastic band stretching in an extreme way, rather than thinking through, getting some advice, and not letting his business mind jump to conclusions, but tactfully approaching this situation with clear and educated thought.

Stay away from impulsiveness and choose purpose and value mixed with your principles. It only takes 30 seconds to refer back to your very own values list. In this man's case, the very thing he was doing in making spontaneous decisions was, in turn, breeding the same behaviors in some of his executive staff. But in 30 seconds I was able to shift his perspective and save him some embarrassment and his reputation.

The key to winning out over an elastic conscience is to take 30 seconds to ask yourself:

1. Does this have my best interest in mind? (Does it support my cause or purpose?)

2. What about my company's best interest, my family's, or another human being's?

3. What about the benefit of my physical health in mind and body?

In real-life situations, where we all have a propensity to react, it's then and there you must hit the pause button and think to yourself, *You are going to achieve your goal of losing weight, and this ice cream is not included in it!* Or, *Brain, stop thinking those thoughts. You know what the truth is!* Really think about the outcome before you act! As you apply your *self* to self-control, you'll be amazed as you watch your body refrain from thinking with an elastic conscience to a mind that is set on achieving anything—be it physical, financial, emotional, mental, or spiritual.

A person with character makes decisions on principle and values, not on the basis of what is popular or what may feel good.

Ron Kardashian

Training and enhancing your conscious mind is challenging. It is difficult but extremely beneficial. Many people who amass wealth and wear Brioni or handmade Italian suits need to open their eyes to see it's not the suit that makes the person but the person behind the fine fabric. You may be wearing handmade Guccis, but even the finest leather sole won't do you any good unless the direction in which your feet are taking you is a path of honor. All these material garments are forms of excellence, I know: I respect fine fabric and beautiful shoes because I love excellent things and attention to detail. However, I want you to think about first developing yourself to be dressed with balance and discipline, living, honestly thinking noble thoughts, and living in peace with that still, small voice. This takes great focus and attention, but it's worth it for anyone who aspires to be the best. There is a price to pay, but you have no other choice if you want to succeed. Do your best in private, and your public life will be strengthened!

Just because you think something in your head does not mean you have to believe it, act on it, or even speak it out of your mouth. In fact, if you're like most human beings, you couldn't answer every thought even if you tried! That's because thoughts come and go all day, every day.

Anything in life can be achieved successfully when it's done with repetition and excellence. By combining the two you can birth greatness.

Ron Kardashian

The key to success is to harness your positive thoughts and use them to make increasingly powerful decisions. How? By thinking it through and converting those positive thoughts into action. Every time you decide to go to the gym, you choose to increase your life span. Every time you decide to fry, zap, nuke, or slather your food with fattening substances instead of eating healthy, fresh, and nutrient-dense food, you choose to decrease your life span.

Decisions are cumulative. The bad decisions you make today make it easier for you to make bad decisions tomorrow. The bad decisions you make tomorrow, in turn, make it easier for you to make even more bad decisions the day after tomorrow. It's a little like debt. You start with a small debt because it's easier to charge something you don't really need on a piece of plastic than to admit that you can't really afford it. As a result, a little debt grows to a larger debt, a larger debt grows to a massive debt, and eventually the debt is so big that your mind is really troubled. Most people bail out and go bankrupt and have to start all over again. However, I don't advocate this type of system. When we give in to negative thoughts and don't face our problems, and instead bury them deep, we create a cumulative atmosphere that makes it easy for us to make worse decisions with every passing day.

The more unresolved anger, emotion, regret, insecurity, anxiety, and resentment we keep in our hearts, the easier it is for us to "blow our stack" and react emotionally rather than logically. For instance, if you are constantly frustrated with your coworkers, the office atmosphere, your workload, your pay, and so on, and you choose not to do anything about it, is it any wonder that one day you suddenly blow up at your manager or boss and ultimately lose your job?

Likewise, if you're unhappy in your relationship but choose to say nothing about it and instead suffer the slings and arrows of emotional and verbal abuse, is it any wonder you eventually "blow" and say—or do—something you'll ultimately regret? That's why you must think it through. Take 30 seconds and ask yourself these three questions prior to making rash decisions:

1. Does this have the best interest of others in mind?

2. Does this have my best interest in mind?

3. Does this decision breed life or death; enhance my destiny and the world in which I live?

Your thoughtful, honest answers to these questions have the power to majorly change your destiny, which is why pushing your own pause button and thinking it through is so important.

WINNING BY DEGREES

The sooner you stop to think about your decisions before you make them—even if it means talking openly and honestly about your situation—the sooner you start making better decisions each and every time. Again, it's winning by a matter of degrees. Just as making bad decisions often leads to making worse decisions, when you begin making better decisions by thinking about your plan of action more and more carefully, this soon leads to making better and better decisions.

It's a little like quitting smoking; not only do you stop smoking, but the minute you do, the body starts healing and undoing all the years of damage caused by smoking. Health experts say that you essentially get a new liver every six months; a new kidney every four months.

Your body is constantly repairing itself, and the brain is no different. The sooner you start making good, thoughtful, valid decisions; the sooner you start undoing the years of damage done by making bad decisions in the first place. Your body's natural propensity is to repair and heal itself. The body will restore itself naturally as long we let it. The heart beats, we breathe, we blink, and we generate new cells. Every second something powerful is happening in the body to heal and restore. The body will heal if we let it. But that is your choice.

GOOD DECISIONS ARE
THE GATEWAY TO CHANGE

The choices you make in life will do one of two things: make you or break you. Life is up to you; nobody else. You decide; it's your move. I want to reiterate and seal the deal that you are the most influential person you are going to meet today! We spend all our lives looking to this person or that for solace, support, and satisfaction, when all along we can find these qualities within ourselves.

What you believe is what you will and must become. There are no substitutes for your belief system. In other words, you can't fake what you believe. It is who you are; it defines you. And it's been that way since you were a very young child. Change is hard. Those 35,000 to 60,000 thoughts we have each day are not only mostly negative but they're also echoes of what we've been thinking our entire lives.

If you think you're not good enough to get that promotion at forty, it's usually because of a series of rejections you've encountered at ten, fifteen, twenty, twenty-five, thirty, and thirty-five. So your negative self-thoughts have sapped your self-confidence over years of rejection.

The coach who told you that you weren't good enough to make the team, the prom date who decided to go with the star basketball player instead of you, the mom who told you that you could "stand to lose a few pounds"—all these rejections lead to our inner thoughts, and unless we mentally try to stop them, these are the thoughts we hear over and over and over again throughout our lives. Change will take effort and time, and more effort and more time, but it will be so worth it in the long run.

If you want to change your life, change your thoughts! You have the power to make or break your life. Every thought is a seed. Feed the good, starve the bad. Pursue the good and ignore the bad. This knowledge is the power to life's greatest successes.

You can't simply "unthink" years of rejection and insecurity. What you can do is get to the point where you stop thinking of limitations and start seeing opportunities. Failures are not fun, I once heard someone say, but they can be fruitful. In other words, the experience you get when you undergo trials manifests lessons that otherwise might never have been learned.

Instead of dwelling on what you have gone through and all the things that have gone wrong, gain power from the experience. When you think like this, you'll rise up as a stronger and more confident person. This is why it is so important to talk to, read about, listen to, and hang out with positive, uplifting, inspirational, wise, and seasoned people who can literally help affect the way you think about life truths and experiences.

MOVING UP AND OVER: YOU ARE (ALREADY) SUCCESSFUL

The only way a boat begins to sink is by letting what's on the outside get on the inside. The same can be said about failure. Keep what you have gained in life through various experiences; let go of what you have lost. It's over, it's done, and the sooner you move on, the sooner you achieve what's known as success. I had a mentor who said that in every experience we have, every book we read, and every person we meet is a means by which we gain experience. It either makes you sharper and stronger or teaches you to avoid it in the future. So in every experience, we can leave behind what we did wrong but keep the experience in our minds to avoid repeating it.

Success is a relative term, defined by each individual on the planet. Some won't consider themselves successful until they're millionaires; others are happy just finding a job. Likewise, your definition of success—how you measure and calibrate what *you* call "success"—changes over time. And it is okay to define success any way you see fit.

What satisfied us when we were twenty may not be as professionally or personally satisfying when we are thirty, to say nothing of forty or fifty. And guess what? *All of this is good!* You, however, can get better at thinking through things. I'm living proof! Today I'm thinking clearer about what I eat, what I achieve, and what I want to be for my wife and kids, for my clients, and for the world.

An important part of the process of thinking clearly is to try to maintain a constant state of humility, which is just basically acknowledging that we don't know everything, that we still have much to learn, and that we're not always right. It also means that we listen to people on a deeper level. You get smarter when you listen with intensity. The fact that we have been given two ears and one mouth might be instructive to think about!

I've known many people who've succeeded for many years, only to fail big-time and have to start all over again. Likewise, I've known many people who struggle all their lives and never quite consider themselves a success—ever—no matter how much wealth or accomplishment they amass. What took a client of mine thirty years to build was lost in a 30-second act of rage—remember Jimmy?

But success isn't in your bank account, driveway, jewelry box, or street address; it's in your perspective and the thoughts you think every moment of the day. Wouldn't you agree that spending a little more time developing your thoughts around grace, peace, the betterment of others, dreams, personal achievements, and making the world a better place would be beneficial?

Think how much the world would change if we restored some basic thought processes (which would then affect our behavior), such as respecting others, being kind, and doing things with honor and dignity. All you need to do is take a 30-second pause and think about what it's like when someone treats you like this, and your ability to do for them as you would want them to do for you is achieved. I believe you can really do this. You are a success story already.

THE 30-SECOND THINKER:

"I'm going to exercise forgiveness. What's done is done! It's over, and I'm moving on. I am filled with thoughts that bring the choicest words and the best actions into the world."

Take time to think about your next major decision in life. Stop thinking of the past—it's over! It hinders you from moving forward. Forgive and move on. Let people off; let them go. Perhaps you have a dream to start your own business, design clothing, pick up art again, fall in love, or make a few million more dollars. Whatever it may be, start to turn your negative self-talk into positive encouragement. Circumstances will change, but your response to those circumstances will remain forever. Slow down and learn to practice thinking positively, with power and purpose.

CHAPTER 3

Speak Precisely:
Put Your Mouth on a Diet

A man will be satisfied with good by the fruit of his words.

Proverbs 12:14 (NASV)

Science has proven that your brain is actually physically affected by the words you speak and the verbal attitudes you express on a daily basis. Your brain is made up of a series of intricate connections between brain cells. These connectors are called synapses. Much the same way your modem connects you to the Internet, these synapses connect one brain cell to another.

Imagine a vast network of humming synapses conveying important messages, just like conversations on phone lines, and you'll get an idea of how the brain physically operates. As brain cells need to communicate with each other, they use these synapses—or connections—to send messages throughout your body to evoke appropriate responses, hence the term "body language."

Research has revealed that half of the synapses you are born with begin to die off by the time you are ten years old. But never fear, there are still about 500 billion synapses left to last the rest of your life. The brain is amazingly economical when it comes to the number of synapses it needs. The more you use them, as you do early in life when every message is fresh and new, the more synapses you have. The less you use them, as we do in later life when our knowledge base is established and we receive or acknowledge more messages, the fewer synapses we need.

It is believed that the reason there are so many synapses at birth is so the infant and young child can have a mental boost to receive input and adapt to the environment in which he or she is born. To a child, of course, everything is learned by example; from sunlight to green grass, from a hot stove to a cold floor, and the way you treat others in front of them, babies continually process all this new information, which is why they need twice as many synapses as the average adult.

Scientists have discovered that these synapses are activated and altered by two main stimuli: chemical substances and words. That's right—words. Using various technological-imaging devices that depict the brain in 3-D, doctors have observed how the brain processes thoughts and various drugs.

My wife was raised in a home where domestic violence was prominent. She has taught me that having heated arguments around our kids is not acceptable. At first I thought, *Big deal.* But once again, my wife was right. We have never had violence in our home, but I have coached several families that have, and even if it's not physical abuse, mental abuse can be just as damaging. Children who have witnessed family violence are affected in ways similar to children who are physically abused. Children in these situations are often unable to establish nurturing bonds with either parent.[6]

It has been shown that children are at greater risk for abuse and neglect if they live in a violent home. In fact, statistics show that more than 3 million children witness violence in their home each year. Children who hear or actually witness violence in the home suffer physically and emotionally. According to authors Robert Ackerman and Susan

Pickering, "Families under stress produce children who are under stress. If a spouse is being abused and there are children in the home, the children are affected by the abuse."[7]

A study at the University of California at Los Angeles revealed that behavior therapy produced the same kind of physical changes in the brain that drugs produced. In other words, therapy that focused on language, speech, and the power of words was equally as effective as drug therapy. Scientists call this "the talking cure." UCLA psychiatrist Dr. Lewis Baxter said that this study revealed the power that words have to physically change the brain.[8]

Imagine the power of words having the same effect on your brain as drugs! This is proof that words really do have power and that it is up to us to wield that power responsibly. Apparently, science is catching up with the truth revealed in the Holy Bible: "Life or death is in the power of the tongue" (Proverbs 18:21, KJV). And Jesus Christ declared, "For out of the abundance of the heart the mouth speaketh" (Matthew 12:34, KJV).

INSIDE THE BRAIN

The sound of words spoken in truth and love is literally music to the heart and mind. Words also affect the health of the physical body and, as we have seen so far, the brain. It is a scientific fact that your brain functions are affected by the sound of words and the images those words produce.

In particular, infants not only respond to words, but words actually help form or "build" the human brain. In his book *Inside the Brain,* Ronald Kotulak writes, "We didn't know that spoken language is such a powerful brain builder." Kotulak also claims scientists recently discovered that a lack of words can stunt an infant's forming brain. It also makes a difference if the words are spoken with love and have meaning to the parent or caregiver. Words coming from a television or radio did not make as much impact on the infant's brain, according to the study.

Scientists have also discovered that the number of words an infant hears each day dramatically boosts intelligence, as well as the ability to socialize. Imagine being able to positively influence your child's future simply by talking to him or her more often and from the heart!

It also appears that language is imprinted in the newly forming brain of an infant very quickly. Apparently, babies learn the sounds of their native language by the age of six months, and they attach meanings to the words of their language by the time they are just one year old.

In short, words have a tremendous impact on the human

brain from the time of birth onward. This means that what you say to others, particularly young children and even infants, has an immediate, specific, and long-term impact. When children do finally begin to speak, they will declare what they have heard, and what they declare will form their lives.

KILL THE NEGATIVITY BEFORE IT BREEDS

Want to know what the single most important voice in the world is? The one you hear when you speak to yourself! Therefore, it's vital that you kill the negativity before it breeds. Have you ever woken up to a beautiful morning— the sun shining, the sky blue, the day like a blank slate in front of you—just waiting to magically be written and then . . . and then . . . the negative self-talk begins?

Instead of counting your blessings, you may fall prey to negative self-talk:

"I'm too happy; something bad's going to happen!
 I can't stay this way."
"If I was only ten pounds thinner, I'd have the
 perfect sundress to wear today!"
"It's going to be one of those days. . . . I wish
 I had a beautiful job to match . . ."

"If only I had someone to share this day with,

　　but I'm too ugly to find a mate!"

What a waste of a golden opportunity to enjoy a beauti-ful, blissful, positive day! In order to be successful, you have to be conscious of your words and purposefully rid yourself of the negative self-talk. *What you speak to yourself is the single most important voice in the world.*

Let's take those same four negative comments and see how positive self-talk could literally turn around how you experience the entire day:

"Today is a receiving day! Something wonderful

　　is going to happen to me today!"

"The ten pounds are coming off! I am getting more

　　beautiful and healthier every day!"

"It's a beautiful day; I'm going to use it to find a

　　wonderful job to match . . . good things are

　　coming my way today!"

"I know there is a purpose in me being single,

　　but my dream mate is on the way!"

What you say to yourself matters; it says so much about who you are, and as we've seen, words literally affect brain waves. That's right: negative self-talk equals brain damage!

Give yourself 30-second positive-talk therapy sessions throughout your day and watch your life change gradually. How do you do this? By putting your mouth on a diet and taking a toxic speech sabbatical.

A NEGATIVE-SPEECH SABBATICAL

Do you need to put your mouth on a "diet"? What I mean by this question is just as there are foods that aren't conducive to your health, there are behaviors that are not conducive to your life, and there are words that are so unhealthy that you are going to have to get rid of them *completely*. Some of you have been thinking negatively for so long that nothing positive can come out of your mouth!

You must banish these phrases:

"I'm so fat."

"I'm a failure."

"I always get sick around this time of year."

"I will never be out of debt."

"I'm so ugly."

"That just kills me."

"I'm so stupid."

"I will never be rich."

"I'll never get that account."

"I will always be this way."

"We could never be that big."

"My company could never do that."

"We'll never . . ."

"We can't."

"IMPOSSIBLE!"

Sound familiar? These are all situations where someone is speaking the problem instead of speaking the solution. And guess what? It only takes 30 seconds to change these sentences into positive statements. Did you know that you don't *ever* need to speak any of these negative statements again? What I want you to understand is that words *carry weight*. Really.

Simply put, what goes into your mind will eventually hit your heart and come out of your mouth. By releasing the transforming power of a 30-second truth, you will begin to defeat the lies that have kept you from fulfilling physical, financial, emotional, mental, and spiritual fitness goals. It's very simple if you practice it. In short, the secret lies in speaking the *solution* and to *stop* speaking the problem. So instead of saying, "I'm so fat [problem]," say, "I'm getting better at eating and exercising [solution]."

In the past there have been a lot of studies on the power of self-talk, but now researchers are confirming how the power of words affect your mood: "Only rarely in the past have studies involving self-talk also assessed the awareness and regulation of emotions.[9] However, contemporary approaches to cognitive behavioral therapy emphasize the modification of self-talk or maladaptive thoughts as one important feature in the process of learning to regulate feelings,[10] and researchers are increasingly noting the potentially important role of self-talk in self-awareness and self-regulation."[11]

Let's study your language and see how it has gotten you where you are today. What kind of power do you give your language? The power of life or the power of death? We all want to say life, but ask yourself the following questions and answer them honestly to see if you truly speak on your own behalf:

"Do I have my own best interest at heart when I speak?"
"Do I speak ill of others?"
"Are my words more positive than negative?"
"Do I talk myself up or put myself down?"
"When I speak of dreams, do I give myself permission to
    succeed, or do I talk myself out of even starting
    to dream?"

THE SECRET POWER OF YOUR SPEECH

While it's not always pleasant to face the truth about how we speak to ourselves, we can't truly "speak it through" until we begin to use the power of words for good rather than evil. We have to stop putting ourselves down and start talking ourselves up.

One way to start doing this is to quit giving yourself permission to talk ill of yourself. Stop calling yourself "fat," "stupid," "lazy," "useless," "worthless," or the dozens of other negative terms you use to describe yourself 1,001 times each day.

Instead, speak with positive, helpful, inspiring language. Remember that not only do your words have meaning but they also have power. When you speak poorly or negatively about yourself, your mind begins to believe what you tell it. So if you're an extremely negative person, you can begin to alter those negative thoughts in seconds by speaking quality words about yourself. It can take time to fully appreciate the power of human speech, but there's no time to begin like the present! I'll start by sharing with you the true secret to harnessing the power of self-talk and speech in one word: control.

If you're going to be successful at anything in life, it's going to take some control, and not only in how we speak to ourselves but also how we speak to others and about others. One of the most powerful forces of human language is the way in which our words affect others. Sometimes the best answer is to say nothing.

Think of the pain you've felt in your own life when others called you names like "fat," "gay," "ugly," "stupid," "useless," or worse. Chances are, the minute you hear these words, you are transported back to the very faces and names of the people who called you them and the places it occurred. Such is the power of negative language.

Not only does it hurt when others call us names, but it also causes us to take that pain and internalize it, unconsciously adopting those characteristics—fat, lame, ugly, stupid, worthless—in our own negative self-talk. Unfortunately, the power of negative self-talk can have the same effect: the more you use positive words to craft your life vision, dreams, and goals, the more power you give to accomplishing them. Likewise, the more negative words you use to describe yourself, your life, your surroundings, your job, or your spouse, the more power you give to sabotaging—or even destroying—your dreams.

Now think about how you talk to others. You could be robbing them of their true power by subtly, maybe even subconsciously, cutting them down. Maybe you don't even realize you're doing it. Let's say your coworker Phil is a little on the chunky side and announces on Monday that he's joining a gym and cutting his food intake in half.

While you may be supportive of Phil losing weight and getting into better shape, do the words you speak actually reflect this positive belief? Maybe you persist in calling him "Big Phil" even as he begins to lose weight.

You might think it's a joke or an incentive for him to keep losing weight; I doubt Phil feels the same way. Or maybe even though you know Phil wants to lose weight, you urge him to join you for a fatty lunch at the local deli, even egging him on by saying, "Come on, Phil; supersize it. What's a few calories, anyway?"

The fact is, your words are directly affecting Phil's success, and not in a positive way. By using a hurtful nickname and referring to Phil as "Big Phil" or any other pejorative term, by suggesting fatty foods instead of healthy ones, you are subtly, possibly unconsciously, sabotaging Phil's success, word by word by word. However, a soft and respectful "You've got what it takes" is a classy way to encourage him.

It might not seem like much at the time, but the power of words is cumulative; it builds up with each instance. So the more you call him names, the fatter Phil feels. The more you tempt him with birthday cake in the break room or with a drive-through lunch, the less likely he is to succeed on his own.

The good news is that with a little control, you can have a direct impact on your life, your business, and the lives of others simply by choosing your words more carefully. Instead of using negative nicknames, give people names that create life, that empower and inspire. Instead of using your words to suggest fast food, fried food, or just plain bad food, take a few extra seconds and use them to suggest a healthier alternative instead. When clients come into my clinic or we do coaching over the phone, for the full hour they hear nothing but life-giving words.

Those whose conversation lacks depth make up for it in length. Choose words of power and your energy will be restored.

Ron Kardashian

I have clients who come in so beat up by their spouses, friends, coworkers, and themselves that by the time our conversation is over, they *all* say, "I feel so much better, I'm ready to conquer the world. I can do anything!" Here's my secret: I take 30 seconds before they come in and say to myself, *Think about the day your clients could have had. Treat them as if they were walking into the Four Seasons Hotel. Lay out the red carpet for them. Be sensitive, kind, thoughtful. Activate love, honor, gentleness, and peace—then speak life!*

You got it. I actually say this to myself. In fact, I coach customer-service reps to do the same. If the service you provide others is not the way you want to be treated, you're limiting the growth of yourself and the company you work for—or run. Controlling your language and learning to speak positively is vital to a long and prosperous life as well as excelling in your workplace. Here are three important tips:

• Listen to yourself: It sounds fairly obvious, but often we talk and don't even really hear what we're actually saying. The next time you're speaking with people at home, at work, or just at the grocery store, don't necessarily censor what you say but *do* consciously listen to your words for at least five minutes. I use this exercise with my clients all the time, and usually they are freaked out by what they hear when they stop and spend just five minutes listening to what they say.

- Get out of the verbal fast lane. Is there any good reason to talk so fast, so often? One of the side effects of our cultural "rapid speak" on cell phones and even in face-to-face conversation is that we often say what we don't mean simply because we're working so hard to keep up. Get out of the verbal fast lane and slow down when you talk. Get into the habit of talking more slowly and you will buy yourself time to say better, wiser, more positive things more often—guaranteed.

- Speak as you would be spoken to. If you doubt how many positive things you say, or don't say, try speaking as if you were on the receiving end. Would you call yourself fat? Stupid? Lazy? A loser? Okay, even if you would or you do use such negative self-talk, ask yourself this: How do you feel when you or someone else calls you a name, puts you down, or tells you that you "can't" or "won't" succeed? Pretty rotten, huh? So the next time you open your mouth, pretend you're on the receiving end and speak accordingly.

DON'T BE A TOXIC HOARDER

By now you may feel you have come to terms with some of the issues in your heart. Now it is time for you to come to terms with them and put them to use with your mouth. Part of the reason we find speaking positively to be such a challenge is that we've been doing it wrong—for years. Think of all of the negative self-talk that's built up over the years; it's like junk in your attic. Every year, rather than cleaning it out and hauling all that stuff to the trash, we just pile more in because it's easier to shut the door and forget it than take it down and deal with it.

Have you ever seen one of those "hoarder" shows, where people can barely move around their homes because they have accumulated so much trash, junk, and unnecessary items that their health, even their safety, is now at risk? That's how our minds are when we clutter them with self-talk and allow negativity to reign.

Our brains need to be free and uncluttered to process the thousands of daily thoughts we have; the more negativity that builds up, the less room we'll have for new thoughts, change, hope, dreams, and *you*.

REPLACE BAD THOUGHTS WITH STRONG, POWERFUL, SEASONED WORDS

Trying to fight thoughts with thoughts won't work. We're not talking about positive thinking as much as we're talking about "life-giving speaking." Words give life or take it away. When you are being mentally tormented by horrible thoughts, don't just think something positive, counter the negative thought with positive, spoken words. Say, "I take authority over that thought. I highly doubt you! I have a sound mind, one of power and authority. I'm going to make it! I am vibrant, intelligent, and a wonderful human being!" *Speak out loud!*

Stop letting your mouth get the better of you; stop cluttering your mind with negativity and downer self-speak. Learn to practice control when you talk, follow my tips for gaining more control over your mouth, and take your (verbal) life back! You are your own boss; never forget it! With life or with death, you have the power to create the world you want. If you think you'll succeed, and you speak it to your heart, you will succeed. I'm living proof that it works.

USE THE "I AM" FACTOR

Sometimes people ask me where I get my insight and wisdom, and I boldly say that I read the ultimate bestselling book of all time: *The Holy Bible*. One of my most powerful evidential coaching abilities came from a very famous biblical story that is extremely profound. When I was younger, we read this story over and over, but it was not until twenty years later that

I realized how inappropriately I was using what I call the "I Am" factor. This one chapter will change forever these three letters for you!

Did you know that whenever you tie the words "I am" to your sentence structures you are literally saying that God is this or God is that? When I tell most people this, they are shocked! Why? Because one of God's names is "I AM." While He is spoken of billions of times every day, very few have a sensitive enough ear to hear this. God told Moses to free His Israelite people from slavery while they were under the rule of Pharaoh. When Moses asked God, "If I do go to Pharaoh and ask him to let my people go, who do I tell them sent me?"

God simply replied, "Tell them the 'I AM' sent you." By introducing the "I Am" factor, I am not trying to get overly religious, but I just want to remind you to be respectable and put a higher value on your own identity. When you talk about Him, you are in essence talking about you. Let me give you a perfect example of this. Whenever my daughter leaves for school, I'm always so impressed when she says to me, "I am your little girl and I love you."

It touches my heart so deeply. I want my very being to represent her life everywhere she goes. In essence, my daughter and I are one; she represents a part of our family, she is a reflection of me and my wife. It's an honor to have her represent our family. I know God thinks the same way about us.

God is large enough to cover when we make mistakes and assumes the responsibility of His name by allowing us to use His name. It's awesome when you come to terms with this and have your own "aha!" moment. I have over 150 "I Am" statements now. Try creating your own "I Am" list like the one below and begin to say these things every day. Whether you believe in God or not, if you put this "I Am" secret to work in your life, you will watch things begin to shift. Say your "I Am" statement out loud:

- **I Am kind to others.**
- **I Am a business owner.**
- **I Am getting in the best shape of my life.**
- **I Am getting better at . . .**
- **I Am beautiful.**
- **I Am a giver.**
- **I Am debt-free.**
- **I Am above my circumstances.**
- **I Am a confident person.**
- **I Am a great spouse.**
- **I Am getting a new job.**
- **I Am losing weight.**
- **I Am handsome.**

- **I Am a money magnet.**
- **I Am gifted.**
- **And so and so on . . .**

Make yourself an "I Am" list. Upload it to your iPhone or iPad or other mobile device and make sure you read and state your list every day; if not daily, do it every three days. This is a sure way to begin the healing process of new belief systems about you that may have taken root over the years. By bringing in a supernatural consciousness, you can expect supernatural results and manifestations.

PATIENT, HEAL THYSELF: A CASE STUDY IN SELF-COUNSELING

Even when you're trained in the art of positive self-talk, letting your guard down and reverting to old ways of negativity and down-speak can quietly seep in if you're not careful. At least, that's what happened to me and my wife, Tia.

My mouth happened to be the central issue that was completely out of control in my relationship with Tia. The answer to my marital problems was right under my nose! It was then that I made the decision to seek counseling. During the first session with the counselor, I sat there thinking,

What am I doing here? How did I get to the place where this was neces-sary? I thought I knew it all!

Then Tia began to open up about the way I was talking to her. I was shocked by what I heard that day—not only that I wasn't perfect when I opened my mouth but, in fact, that just the opposite was true. That was the day I discovered that my words hurt Tia and, in fact, often scared her. My wife had reached a point in our relationship where she was afraid to discuss certain problems with me because of what my reaction might be.

Whew! I had no idea that my words were affecting her so negatively. In all my "talk" about positive speech and using the right words, I had been oblivious to her feelings and the impact my attitudes were having on our marriage.

Then I remembered that there is creative power in our words, power for death or life. I also remembered some of the things I had said to her—and to others. I realized that too many times I had spoken terrible things to someone I loved so much.

I felt like the person who declares as "one who speaks rashly like the thrusts of a sword" (Proverbs 12:18, KJV). How I longed for the second part of that proverb to become my reality: "But the tongue of the wise brings healing."

During those sessions, I discovered that I had to learn to love myself so that I could love Tia the way I wanted to love her and the way she deserves to be loved. In practical terms, that meant I had to change the way I spoke about myself and about her, as well as the way I talked to her and other people.

I was speaking disrespectfully because I had no respect for myself. This was a hard reality to learn. As I gained understanding, I began to learn to speak the truth from my heart, kindly, in love. My self-respect and my respect for my wife grew immeasurably with the acceptance of this powerful experience I am coaching you through.

Similarly, it may also be a hard reality to learn what is holding you back, such as a struggle losing weight and getting into shape. Perhaps you need to learn to respect yourself, as I did. Meditating on your vision statement and declaring it to be the reality you want to live will help you to go forward toward the freedom you desire. (I will show you how to write a vision statement a little later.)

Respect for yourself, your life, and your regimen for improved health must be a high priority for your life, just as my marriage is for me. In both situations, our mouths have everything to do with the outcome. Whether we are considering the words we speak and how we speak them (what comes *out* of our mouths) or the food we eat (what we put *into* our mouths) the answer to our freedom is right under our nose.

That day in the counselor's office was the day I started on a new journey in learning to talk right, which taught me a lot about how to help my clients—and you—become people who can fulfill their dreams.

Of course, my marriage is a journey for life. Learning to communicate with my wife and watching our love grow as a result is a daily process. It is wonderful when I succeed and painful when I fail. But it is giving me unlimited compassion for you! So I am choosing my words carefully as I write, because I want you to reach your God-given potential in every area of your life, and particularly in your personal life, health, and financial needs.

The entire time I attended those marital coaching sessions, I couldn't help thinking that while I had learned that by controlling my mouth I could get my body and life into shape, it was my mouth that was actually making my marriage and parenthood worse. The words of my mouth had indicated to my wife that I did not love her. I really did not know the bad effect my words had on her psyche.

Words changed the atmosphere that afternoon, and I never forgot this powerful lesson.

THE IMPORTANCE OF INTEGRITY

Integrity is a word that has majorly affected my life and my coaching practice. And it's a 30-second thought process. At some point, you're either going to choose to do things the right way or continue to do them wrong. I know firsthand, because in my teens I was *not* a man of integrity; in striving daily to be that man, I found integrity to be my lifeline for a true and thoughtful path and very successful financial, marital, physical, and spiritual life. Integrity is more than just being truthful, honest, and reliable with others; it's being all those things to yourself! For some reason, it's much easier for me to be honest with others then with myself.

Take texting while driving, for example, which is something I did without thinking twice about it. But when I learned of its dangers, I promised my wife—and then Oprah—that I would not text on the road.

Notice I didn't say I wouldn't text in the car, but at least now I pull the car over. That was a hard one for me. I only achieved it by getting in what I call "integrity shape." That's right; you need to exercise your integrity muscle. It's the proof of the genuine soul that longs for excellence.

I like to call it the "deal maker" or the "deal breaker" and might I add, choosing to act with integrity is a *30-Second Solution* that counts—big time. Integrity is made up of two very important factors:

1. What you do
2. What you say

When these two factors collide, they make up the concept of integrity. At some point or another, we have all met people who have promised to be at a certain place at a certain time and never showed up. How did that make you feel?

Abandoned? Let down? Upset?

Anyway, it's not a good feeling. Whenever we fail to meet the same expectations in our own actions the reverberation echoes throughout our lives; and in one way or another, it negatively affects our lives.

To live your life in a successful way, place a high demand on your integrity. It's the one area of your life in which you will leave a legacy for the people after you. This principle is vital to a company's success. Making promises to clients and not keeping them is an integrity issue. Saying you will pay on time and not doing so, at least without a 30-second e-mail, fax, or letter, is a lack of integrity. No excuses!

You want to make it big and get to the top? Your skill set may get you there, but only character and integrity will keep you there. I'm the type of person and coach who not only wants to affect the world but also wants to be honorable and full of integrity while getting there.

I want wealth not only for what I can acquire but also to supply a wealth of knowledge to a world in need. When you give from a heart that desires leaving a legacy of integrity, wealth takes on new meaning. Give from a heart that longs for truth and promise, rather than a heart that wants to be recognized for doing charitable acts. If you're giving and wanting others to see you give, that's fine, but don't you think it would be just as good if you give *without* anyone seeing?

Integrity means doing good deeds, even when no one is looking. Work at telling yourself, even saying it out loud: *I have a heart that is open and yearns for truth. I want to get better, not bitter. I want to be wealthy and wise. I want to be a person of integrity.*

To be true to yourself, watch out for these statements:

- "We will *always* be poor . . . in debt . . . in this mess!"
- "I will *always* be fat."
- "I am a nothing." (Remember the "I Am" secret.)
- "*Nobody* likes me."
- "I will *never* be a beautiful as he or she."
- "At this rate I will *never* be happy or married."
- "I will *never* be that successful . . . or get out . . ."
- I am *not* as talented as. . . . "
- I am *not* genetically gifted like them."
- "I will *never* get that job."

Do some of these phrases sound familiar? I hear them every day, coming out of the mouths of clients who you would never imagine would feel this negatively about themselves.

While *all* words have meaning, some words are frankly more harmful than others. Take another look at the sentences above, paying special attention to the italicized words; they are just some of the dozens of words I've identified that do serious "brain damage" to otherwise healthy people.

These words are damaging whether spoken to family members, friends, or a coworker. As a coach for a U.S. company, I interviewed employees and asked them how they liked their jobs and what would they do differently if they had a voice. An executive team leader told me he found it disturbing when the CEO paced the hallways cursing and throwing out defeatist remarks about his own company! The CEO was shifting the atmosphere of the entire building while his team was looking for leadership. The employee told me, "Please tell him to stop it; it's really affecting all of us who are working so diligently. It's fighting against us!" Unfortunately, this story does not have a good ending. I did tell the CEO to stop his ranting, but he did not listen. As a result, his ship is continuing to sink, because the captain is speaking defeat rather than victory.

SPEAK THE SOLUTION, NOT THE PROBLEM

To speak positively, you have to eliminate the negative language from your vocabulary. By eliminating the negative verbal clutter, you leave room for the positive, the upbeat, and the inspirational. Try to practice eliminating the old and learning to hit the "refresh" button on your mouth. Practice thinking with dignity and respect through your words prior to letting them off like a machine gun. If you mess up, don't worry. Just take 30 seconds and start again. Catching yourself making a mistake is the only way you're going to get it right.

Remember that a wise person will fall seven times but get up eight. You'll see that in time, when you speak with positivity, people will see a new side of you and will look forward to being with you. In time, your career will prosper, your relationships will improve, and your health will turn around. When I began writing this book and sharing the vision of it with others, every person I shared it with said the same thing, "Ron, you're right; seconds do matter!" The fact is, every thirty seconds you have a choice: to say something positive or to say something negative. Likewise, if you think you'll fail and you say it out loud enough times, guess what? You will fail. Case in point: I know a guy who was always saying he would never live past forty. Folks, he died at thirty-nine! Words carry weight. Remember to speak the solution, not the problem.

30 SECONDS TO 20 MILLION

One of my favorite business success stories involves a company that I coach abroad. The CEO sought me out to help him keep his new company thriving, increase revenue, and maintain balance in his life. At the time, he was about fifty pounds overweight and was earning about $750,000 per year. When I first began coaching him, he was very optimistic, but every once in a while, certain fears would surface, thoughts that we all get concerning failure, such as *Did I do the right thing? Are we going to make it? How is this going to get done? What if this happens? What will they think of me?*

My coaching was pure empowerment, not only by encouraging aggressive business strategies and infrastructure to ward off those attacks, but to keep him on point. One day I asked him this question: "Are you going to give life to those fears by telling all your employees what you are facing, or are you going to speak the *solution* to those fears?" Then I added, "Your employees are not looking for a weak, frail, emotional basket case in a CEO! As a leader, rise up and *speak the future* of the company!" I really lovingly yet powerfully let him have it—in all of 30 seconds!

Well, I thought he was going to jump through the phone. I would like to remind all you entrepreneurs or people with start-up companies who are seeking funding about this powerful advice I gave to him next: "When you went to the venture capital firm and asked for money, you conveyed your vision with crystal clear words, and, of course, projections, the return on invested capital, and all the business elements. But ultimately, they invested in *you*, not just the technology or the company." People can sense fear and a feeling of failure.

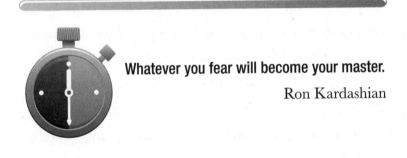

Whatever you fear will become your master.

Ron Kardashian

His reply was shocking. "You're absolutely right! I owe it to myself and the ones who invested in me!" Since then we have walked through many corporate and personal storms together, but now this award-winning CEO is down forty-seven pounds, and a *billion*-dollar company is considering acquiring him for $10 to 20 million! Friends, if you think words don't matter, you're in trouble and so is your company!

YOUR WORDS CAN CHANGE YOUR THINKING

Chances are, your whole life you've heard negative things, whether in boardrooms, bedrooms, or classrooms. If you're like most people reading this book, the majority of the things you say to and about yourself are, for the most part, negative. Maybe you celebrate an achievement with some self-praise or mental pats on the back, but for the most part, the human condition is such that negativity rules—and positivity is out.

What we have to do is switch the focus so that it's turned around, with positivity ruling and negativity forced out. Unfortunately, you can't just toss negativity out the window and replace every bad word, thought, or phrase with something positive. That's like turning a speedboat on a dime. Weaving positivity back into your life—and into your mouth—is more like turning the *Titanic*; you start immediately and hope you can turn in time before crashing into the iceberg! In other words, you better start now!

You can "be good" for a weekend and listen for negativity and watch what you say, but if you don't gradually fold that practice into your daily life—if you don't make talking positively a habit—then the "hoarder" in you takes over, and pretty soon your life is cluttered with don'ts, won'ts, shouldn'ts, and couldn'ts, and suddenly, another year of negative energy has gone by.

BE A GENTLEMAN OR A GENERAL, BUT SERIOUSLY: BE GENUINE

Fortunately, I have been working on this "verbal muscle" for a long time, and now it's one of my strongest. Prior to my marriage, I never really thought about what came out of my mouth. If I thought it, I said it. And what came out of my mouth really made some people *mad*. The women I dated became furious. Coworkers were insulted, and family members walked away hurt. For the life of me, I couldn't understand why. Okay, I could understand why, and that's when I realized that I had to stop and think about my words and their impact on others. That's when I became the boss of my own mouth—and life!

With practice and self-control, I stopped using the F-bomb at least ten times per day. I started speaking my financial destiny using positive, success-oriented words instead of negative, failure-centered words. I began speaking the truth about the house I wanted to live in; even the type of man and father I wanted to be.

The one-night stands, my partying friends, and even people I thought were my close friends left me in a heartbeat! While at the time I felt very alone, I decided that instead of spiraling down into self-pity, I'd use the time to improve myself. I exercised and watched inspiring movies, dove into personal-development books and listened to hundreds of hours of gifted professions on life topics, as well as learning how to be comfortable in my own company. I loved the feel-good movies and noticed that all the male characters had one thing in common: they were gentlemen and generals in life, meaning they were gracious yet in control. Men or women who are in control of themselves cannot be stopped or controlled by their circumstances, regardless of what the circumstances are.

One day I actually spoke these words out loud: "Ron, if you're going to do anything with your life, do this: Be a gentleman. Strive for excellence in everything you do. Take control of your destiny." It was literally a 30-second thought process that manifested itself in my life. I was not that man yet, but I sure wanted to be, and today I am farther down the road. I married the woman of my dreams. I have two successful companies, I travel the world, my children honor me, and by speaking with positivity, using words that reflect my true purpose, I have made even more friends than I had before—and better-quality friends who appreciate me and are in alignment with the gifts and callings and cause for which I was created.

YOUR MOUTH CAN GET YOU MARRIED

People always ask me, "Ron, where did you meet Tia? She is so gorgeous, inside and out." I love hearing that question! Personally, I like calling her the hottest of the Kardashian girls. She had no trouble finding any man she wanted. When we met, I was carrying myself as a young single guy on the prowl; my heart was protected by walls, and I was deluding myself that life in the fast lane was what I wanted.

On the other hand, she had men, money, and the mansion, but she, too, felt empty. She wanted a husband and not just any man. When I met her I thought she was married. As it turns out, she was so fed up with dating men, she decided to think like a married woman and started carrying herself that way.

She decided to stop dating and said to herself, *The next man I meet has got to be the one I'm going to marry, and I will not have it any other way.* She then started carrying herself in a completely different way—she changed the way she dressed and flirted. She began a new way of thinking, and as a result, a new way of speaking: "I am going to act like a married woman. How would a married woman walk, talk, represent herself . . . ?" and so on. See why I thought she was married? While some of you may think she went to extremes to secure her goal, our marriage is still going strong. So if you're still single and want to find the one, try this for yourself.

When people ask me, "Ron, how and where did you find each other?" I tell them that a true gentleman is looking for a bride, not a woman for a one-night stand. I was not looking for a young, hot, sexy woman; I was looking for a young, hot, sexy wife—someone to grow old with—which is a big difference. The way we carry ourselves and the way we talk are two very powerful forces that will cause us to attract certain types of people. I'm talking from firsthand experience. When my mouth changed, my life changed, and as you can imagine, my heart changed, by falling in love with the most amazing woman in the world. Of course, my marriage is a journey for life. Learning to communicate with my wife and watching our love grow as a result is a daily process. It is wonderful when I succeed and painful when I fail, but it is giving me unlimited compassion for others.

Have you ever spoken in the heat of the moment and been surprised, for better or worse, by what comes out of your mouth? That is your subconscious speaking directly through your tongue, without the filters we usually apply to our speech.

What people say reveals what they think—the principles they honor, obey, and respect. The fact is, human speech reveals these things whether we're consciously thinking them or not. Language has the power to heal or to harm, and oftentimes we don't know which one we're doing because we simply don't listen to ourselves.

I can tell a lot about a people just by listening to them talk to other people—or to me—for a while. What they say is particularly illuminating when you stop to listen to it closely. The words they use to describe themselves and others, to express their thoughts and feelings, and to describe events and situations says a lot about who they really are inside. I can hear what or who has had the greatest influence on them and understand something of the environment in which they grew up. Their words tell me what they honor. They also reveal whether they are honest. Words impact your brain, emotions, central nervous system, and the life you lead. Now that you know your words have creative power, take pains to listen to yourself with a more enlightened and understanding view.

Up until now, you may not have believed that your own words have such a great impact on your well-being; now you know better. As you hear your own words, challenge yourself to gain insight into what is really going on inside you. Positive thoughts lead to positive actions. This is why when it comes to losing weight, getting a new job, changing your life, changing your career, or bringing your life to another level, you need to think and speak positively. I always say, "Put your mouth on a diet first." If you speak positively, you will act positively.

Hear me when I say this: the words that come out of your mouth are either making you or breaking you. There is no middle ground. If you stop saying, "I'm so fat," the process of weight loss begins. I know it sound too good to be true, but I have seen this firsthand when I did personal training in the gym for over a decade. If you stop speaking words that make you feel like a failure, success begins. If you stop speaking words that make you feel loveless, love begins.

The same principle applies to increasing the amount of money you make every year, to getting out of debt, or finding the mate of your dreams. When Tia and I began changing our mind-sets and the way we spoke, we were in debt with no way out. So we began thinking and talking like people who paid cash. Guess what? That meant we couldn't use our charge cards! In three months we were completely out of debt. This is not magic; it's a discipline that you can learn. With just the few seconds it takes to speak, you can either build life or create more death (or should I say "debt"?).

Take the time to stop and think before you speak and before you make emotional decisions, be it with what you eat or what you buy. The following tips will help you to see that

speaking without thinking is a lot like walking backward—
you waste a lot of time and money and never get where you
really want to go:

- **Be honest with yourself.** The first step to thinking
  positively is to free yourself from guilt, shame, and dis-
  honesty. After all, if you can't be honest with yourself,
  whom can you be honest with?

- **Speak the truth.** You have to speak the truth. No more
  lying to yourself—or to others! Not even little fibs! They
  gotta go! If you can't think the truth, then you won't
  speak the truth. So think long and hard about what the
  truth really is, face it, and then speak it. Trust me, you'll
  be glad you (finally) did!

- **Know your goals.** When you speak, you want to be
  clear about what it is you're seeking—relationship success, losing weight, getting a new job, going back to
  school, spiritual peace, and so on. Speaking what you
  know only happens when you know what to speak!

Don't believe me? Consider the following list of (very)
common phrases uttered hundreds of times a day and see if
they don't sound (way too) familiar:

"I can't do this."

"The economy did this to me."

"I can't lose weight."

"I always fail eventually."

"I will never be able to get that job."

"I was born a loser."

"My problem is genetic."

"I get sick at the same time every year."

"My mom was built like this."

"My dad was built like this."

"I'm too scared."

"No matter how hard I try, it never works."

"I'm so unqualified for this job."

"I have no special talents or gifts."

"I'm not attractive enough to date."

"I'm just not the marrying kind."

"My life isn't meant to be happy and fulfilled."

"I'm just not attractive."

"I have no energy."

"I hate my hair!"

"I don't have any help."

"I am a lost cause."

"It's too late for me."

If any of these statements or similar statements have come out of your mouth, from now on *get rid of them*—and fast!

All of these statements have one deadly effect: they reject the power of good actions to take root in your favor. Don't be your own worst enemy when it comes to success; speak the positive, inspiring, and authentic truth and help yourself help yourself.

WHAT YOU SAY IS WHAT YOU DO: MOUTH FITNESS

Speaking is a skill, and like all skills, it requires practice. It also requires understanding. So know this: what you say is what you do. If you talk about failure, predict failure for yourself, set yourself up for failure with negative words and complaints and lots of don'ts and can'ts, guess what? You will fail. There's simply no way you can succeed if you don't first believe in your success.

You simply have to believe in the potential of what you can create. Stop putting limits on your success, and positivity will follow. I want you to begin by speaking more positively every time you are tempted to "go negative" with your tongue.

We'll start with a simple exercise. Below are negative phrases followed by positive affirmations. Every time you find yourself thinking or saying the negative version, I want you to replace it with the positive statement:

"I can't . . ."

"I *can* begin to . . ."

"I'll always look fat . . ."

"I *can* change my appearance if I want to . . ."

"I'll never be. . . . "

"I *will* do what I said I can do, and I will have what I say I can have!"

"I'm stupid and worthless . . ."

"I *am* a highly favored individual who is filled with more wisdom and understanding."

"I would if I could . . ."

"I *can* do anything I set my thought and mind to."

"Today is a horrible day . . . I woke up on the wrong side of the bed."

"Today *is* going to be a wonderful day. Something great is going to happen to me today."

"It won't ever happen for me . . ."

"I *am* going to expect something good to happen to me!"

Do you see how for every negative phrase there is always a positive alternative that can literally change your future?

And do you see how a lifetime of "I can't," and "I wouldn't," and "I'll never" can lead to a self-fulfilling prophecy by creating a person who can't, won't, and never will succeed? All because you've told yourself you can't!

Tell yourself you *can*! Right now—today—before it's too late and another year, then another, then five, then ten, then twenty years of can't, won't, and shouldn't add up in your brain and you really "can't" become who you were meant to be because you've already got one foot in the grave.

What you say is what you do. So what are you saying? And how can you *do* better by talking better?

VERBALIZE YOUR DREAMS TO OTHERS

While it's important to speak positively to yourself, it's also important to be confident enough in your success that you speak your goals and intentions to other people. Your dreams are powerful things, but no dream can ever come true if you're not confident enough in it—and in your ability to reach it—to say it out loud.

The more often you speak your dreams, the more power you give them. Practice speaking aloud your inspirations, your hopes, and your dreams. It only takes a moment, and watch what happens to your mind! I guarantee that you'll feel the power of the spoken words as they breathe new dreams to life.

From Disney World to Facebook, from *Toy Story* to the iPad, from football to government, everything you see, hear, touch, feel, and spend money on was created via the mouth, which generated reality through an *idea*. That is why *ideas* are the most powerful things in the world, but only if you believe in the power of ideas; because if you don't believe in what you think, you'll never be able to speak your dreams aloud.

Dream dreams and talk about them. I am always telling business leaders that in order for their employees to know what they are thinking and envisioning, the leaders must clearly convey vision. On the other hand, you need to be selective with whom you share your dreams. Remember they are your dreams, and sometimes not everyone can envision your vision. There are also those naysayers and manipulators who want to shoot down your dreams with their words. If that happens, as it happens to all of us, you need to take 30 seconds and remember the truth. Say to yourself out loud, "I don't need to receive that person's comment! I am not going to let it affect me."

REPETITION IS THE MOTHER OF MASTERY

As we wind down the chapter, I want to leave you with one final tool: the joy of repetition. That's right, excelling in the art of speaking also requires repetition. For example, in his book *Outliers: The Story of Success,* Malcolm Gladwell talks about the "10,000-Hour Rule" and says that becoming successful at mastering a skill takes at least 10,000 hours. Think how successful you could be at speaking like a master if you start right now—30 seconds at a time. Just like becoming a great musician or becoming a good athlete in a sport, it takes repetition. But unlike any sport, the fine-tuning of this art is accomplished in short, quick bouts that take seconds to learn and seconds to keep. In short, every time you speak positively, you remove the opportunity for negativity to seep into your language. Additionally, every positive word increases your chances of succeeding, while every negative word decreases those odds.

To master the art of speaking, you must learn the joy of repetition. Repeat what's good about you multiple times per day. Don't be afraid to speak well of yourself; this isn't about ego—it's about your physical, financial, emotional, mental, and spiritual health! Confidence needs to give strength to your words. You exercise that confidence by meditating on your dreams.

Great athletes and musicians are perfect examples of how repetition produces excellence. As a college professor once said to a young up-and-coming basketball player, "Don't just practice your free-throw shot; practice making it in the basket!"

You don't have to be an athlete, a musician, or a celebrity to apply this principle to everything you want to master in life. Become infectious with a positive life. Be contagious with joy. Words change nations when they are spoken with power. Make your life viral. Infect someone else with the power of your positive life and words.

Remember, positive thinking leads to positive speaking, which leads to positive actions and outcomes. The more you practice, the easier it becomes. Eventually, true, authentic, and lasting change will come. Don't let a 30-second "bad-mouth moment" destroy what has taken your whole life to build.

The tongue is the deal maker or deal breaker. Speaking is an art, and when you speak positively, power will flow in your life. What you say to yourself brings the greatest development. You're the boss of you! Be a great one! Say this: "Greatness is within me. I was created for a specific purpose. I am not moved by my circumstances. I handle everything in my life with peace and clarity. Nobody can do my life better than me. I have got what it takes to make it big!"

CHAPTER 4

Act Purposefully:
Action Equals Results!

Faith without works is dead
[rendered powerless or inoperative].

James 2:26 (KJV)

Actions really do speak louder than words. You can think all day about what you should do, and talk all night about what you want to do, but until you actually put some feet to the floor, get up, and do something (i.e., physically act), no change will ever come. Not today, not next week, not next year. And didn't you start reading this book because you really, truly wanted to change and learn better skills for creating solutions?

Newton's Third Law says that for every action, there is an equal and opposite reaction, and that a body that is in motion stays in motion. I love this law because it's truthful and powerful. Once you get going on something, especially something you really want to do in life, it gets easier and more exciting. That's the perspective you need to have to bring about change: you are getting better at life, and life is all about movement.

Average people do what average people do, but millionaires do what millionaires do: and that is doing what most people will never do.

Ron Kardashian

As you are reading this book, the earth is moving. Your body is constantly moving, even when you're sitting still. If the earth were to stop moving, the planet would freeze or burn depending on which side the sun was shining, and oxygen would no longer be available in the atmosphere. Your body is such a powerful reminder of movement. Without you even thinking about it, your body moves automatically—and quite impressively. Check out these impressive statistics:

- On average, you blink once every five seconds. That's equal to 17,000 times each day or 6.25 million times a year.[12]
Your heart pumps about 2,000 gallons of blood per day—around 60 million gallons in a lifetime. That's a pretty powerful action plan.
- An average human breathes approximately 10 times per minute, 600 times per hour, or 14,400 times per day, which adds up to 5,256,000 per year.[13]

These observations remind us just how important the human body is, don't they? Creating the correct action plan for health is vital to making the body last a long time and fulfilling all your dreams and visions. The body actually likes to move. It was designed to move. That's why global obesity has been rising in the past decade—people don't like action and movement. But it's a basic part of who we are as human beings. In this chapter, you're going to learn how to act with your values in mind and get the results you want.

THE KARDASHIAN FAMILY
VALUES THAT MOVE US TO ACT

Values move you into purposeful action and support your cause. There are several values that my wife and I possess. I wear them right on my wedding ring, in a crest I had designed so we can see them every day. It's important for you to instill mutually agreed upon values into your marriage and your children. It becomes a road map when life's atrocities come your way. And, believe me, they will.

I suggest you sit down with your loved ones and ask one another to define the values that are most important to you, and then write them down. Here are some examples of my family's values so we are all on the same page. Don't confuse these family values with our personal values and our corporate values. We have values for everything. While your family values may change over the years, get started today by putting them down on paper. We value:

1. **Love:** God is love. Love of God, self, and others. Love is an attitude not an emotion. It's a state of patience and an inward working of the heart. The way we react to and treat other people must be loving.

2. **Faith:** Believing the best, even when the best cannot be seen. Doing things with belief and hope in people, places, and things.

3. **Honor:** Being honest with ourselves, our bodies, and those in authority. It's a place for dignity where consideration rules, not only for us but for all human life. It includes our character and the integrity in which we walk at home, work, and play.

4. **Kindness:** A conveyance and a disposition. We are gentle in our approach with one another and with those we encounter. This includes speaking kindly of others.

5. **Peace:** An inward state of the spirit, mind, and body. The still, small voice that confirms, leads, guides, and directs our decisions and motivations. No peace—no go!

6. **Wealth:** Stewardship. The inclusion of money and wealth; the ability to provide for the needs of our lives and improve the lives of others. Charity, benevolence. Respect money; don't abuse it. (Most people I know don't value money nor do they teach their children to value it. We raise our children to have a deep gratitude for what we have, combined with an understanding that there are responsibilities that come with privilege and that we should never take for granted anything we have. They are learning that money is a tool, and when used correctly, it can help the world.)

That is the government of our life and my declaration of independence! Without these values, I'd be walking a lonely, senseless, purposeless path in my most valuable calling: the role of husband and father. Remember that values work in any setting. For example, let me show you how values serve as a guideline to propel purposeful action in your personal life, your family life, and your business life.

Let's say my son gets into an argument with a boy at school. How do I give him a 30-second reminder to help him resolve the issue he is facing? The first thing I want him to do is to think about our family values: Is he honoring the first value of love? Is he walking in love? I say, "Son, do you understand this little boy's position?" (For instance, he may not have eaten breakfast this morning, or maybe he was abused before he went to school, etc.)

Will my son have to use some faith or belief that the outcome of this situation will be as it should when he applies our family values to it? Sure, you're darn right. I will need to use some faith, too; I can't see the outcome. This little boy might want to fight or do something immature. But I enforce faith and belief, and friends, when you enforce belief, it becomes powerful.

I'm teaching my little boy how to walk in love in the schoolyard, which is action aligned with our values and purpose.

I'm not telling him to be a pushover; it's about being pushed up, not pushed over. You push me? You're not pushing me over—you're pushing me up! I believe that even when life brings us enemies, with the proper perspective, they can become stepping-stones to a higher level of emotional and spiritual maturity in our lives.

I ask my son, "Did you walk in love? Did you use your faith? Were you honest and kind to him?" To reiterate, we don't know if that little boy was abused before he went to school that morning, or maybe he didn't get breakfast and his glycemic level was low.

Naturally, my children will not comprehend all the specifics all at once. Maybe he won't "hear" me today or tomorrow, but I know that I'm imparting a belief system in him, and as the years go by and I keep encouraging him to walk in love, it will become part of the fabric of his life and teach him to respond in this way, instead of just reacting to the situations that he's in. It's like everything else—a process.

Be the teacher, leading by example, and train your children to be adults. We coach them with love and logic. If you don't, when they get older and are flying off the cuff, it will be your fault to some degree! You have the power to influence and reflect composure; our children are watching us and observing our behaviors. We'd better keep our behaviors backed by values and a belief system that will win their hearts and help them live in a world where conflict is inevitable. We have the power to teach them that although we are not always in control of what happens to us, we are in control of our response to what happens to us. I cannot stress this enough!

The busier you are, the more time you must spend with your kids. I'm not talking about quantity, I'm talking quality. For example, it only takes 30 seconds to say to your teenage daughter, "What's on your mind, sweetheart?" You can say to your son, "I really respect you for the man you have become! Can I take you to a baseball game?" Thirty seconds to make the decision equals a 30-year memory. It angers me when I see businessmen or businesswomen neglecting their families at the cost of big business! The fabric of humanity and growth is found in the upbringing of a generation, not just a corporation. Spend time with your kids, show you value them, and fill them with the wealth of knowledge, guidance, and love.

POWERFUL ACTION

What are the values that compel you to purposeful action in your life? A prolific leader once spoke of a time that he was approached after one of his speaking engagements by a woman who asked him if he did any online coaching. At the time he was not set up to do this type of coaching, but he did value his integrity. His business model was segregated into two dimensions: coaching one-to-one and speaking to large audiences. But his 30-second response to her question ended up skyrocketing his profession and his monthly revenues. He did not abruptly say *no* to her but took 30 seconds to think before he spoke. His reply is a perfect example of how preparedness and willingness to act with a value can alter big business when the moment approaches, and this was his moment. He said, "If I did have an online coaching program, would you be interested in taking it?"

The woman replied, "Of course I would!"

The man then said, "Well, if you can find ten other people at this conference who are interested in an online coaching class, and who will sign up today, I will do a monthly newsletter coaching you online for five dollars a month."

Her reply was, "Great! I'll get the ten at this conference." By the end of the conference, 150 had signed up, and as a result of this 30-second successful response, this man now has more than 150,000 people on his newsletter list. At five dollars a month per subscriber? You do the math. This coach could have been caught up in the moment and stayed stuck in his traditional mind-set of working within his normal business model, but he was willing to act "outside the box." It's not about just *re*acting, but rather about *acting* with power. This is the secret to closing your deal: speak right and be ready to act when opportunity knocks, and the power will flow.

Read this slowly: Do you, at times, find yourself *doing* what you don't want to do and *not doing* what you want to do? It sounds like a tongue twister, I know, but this very real and potentially very damaging dilemma defines almost everyone who is trapped in an unhealthy lifestyle, and it contributes to long-term, repetitive actions that you may later regret. The solution to this problem is simple—but not easy.

Let's look at an example that most of us face on a weekly, if not daily, basis: You want to exercise, but you don't. You don't want to sit around the house and eat junk, but you do. Why? Because the path of least resistance—the path of least action—is much easier to follow than the road to action.

By now we all know what we need to do to lose weight: move more and eat less. So why don't we just do it? Well, because it takes planning to get to the gym after work and still shuttle the kids from practice to practice, extracurricular activity to extracurricular activity. It takes commitment to change and stretch and exercise when it's literally the last thing we want to do after another long, hard day at work. It also takes more time to cook a healthy, tasty, fresh meal than it does to pick up something on the way home or nuke something from the freezer.

That's why I say the solution is simple—just do what you say you're going to do—but far from easy. It's really simple to plan a daily workout routine on paper, but not very easy to stick to it when life gets in the way. The numbers come in at work, so you have to stay two hours late; there goes your workout today! The next day you actually make it to the gym at your prescheduled time, but it takes so long to get ready, find an open machine at rush hour, then shower and change before you're due to pick up the kids that, well, your one-hour workout turns into about twenty minutes of actual physical movement. And so it goes.

The problem is that this happens for years and years at a time. Every week it's the same story; every month, it's the same story. Every year you find yourself disappointed with your progress—or lack of progress. It's not just going to the gym, eating right, or losing weight; it's everything that's tough, challenging, or even rewarding that we want in our lives.

Do you do what you don't want to do, and don't do what you want to do? We can apply this question to all the areas of our lives: our careers, our education, our finances, our relationships, even our search for purpose and happiness.

We don't necessarily "want" to just date or have a one-night stand, but we do it anyway, even though what we really want to do is have a meaningful (and maybe long-term) relationship. We don't save any money out of our paycheck this week, even though what we really want to do—and planned on doing—is to put away 10 percent off the top each week. We don't ask our boss for that big raise, even though we know we deserve it.

And on and on it goes. Does this sound familiar yet? If so, it's because most of us ignore what we want to do in favor of what our inner selves have confirmed and reiterated is important for us to do. We know it's important to save money, but it's so much easier to spend it. We know it's important to remain faithful in our relationships, but it's so easy to _____ (you fill in the blank). Action requires commitment, because when we commit ourselves to something, we hold ourselves accountable for making that "something," whatever it may be, happen.

Even if you've thought everything through completely and know exactly what needs to be done, if you don't put those thoughts into action, nothing will come of it. Likewise, if you "talk the talk" ("I'm going to lose ten pounds by summer," "I'm going to save 10 percent of each paycheck and put it into savings," "I'm committed to faithfulness in my marriage"), but don't "walk the walk," all of these words are like feathers in the wind.

But here's the great news: As you apply positive actions to your life day after day, your desires will start to change, because you will experience the positive outcome those new desires bring. You will want more of the good and healthy things and less of the unpleasant and unhealthy things. In short, you will do more of what you want to do and less of what you don't want to do.

ACTION: IT'S EASY, AND ALL IT TAKES IS ONE

Here is how I want you to begin: just pick one thing you've wanted to do and do it. It really is that simple. It doesn't have to be a "big" thing, either, like going back to school, switching careers, or losing fifty pounds. As you move forward, it doesn't matter if it's a molehill or a mountain—all change begins with a single action and a single choice. Or, as Lao-tzu so famously said, "A journey of a thousand miles begins with one step." What step are you going to take today toward changing your life today?

Millions of Americans want to change, and this is how I have coached thousands of people. One simple 30-second action, repeated, can lead to huge results if you simply start right now and commit to acting on that one particular thing. I'm going to level with you: these are the tools and the solutions, but you must talk honestly to yourself—and stop doing nothing. Not choosing to change is a very powerful choice. It means that you have chosen to always be the way you are. If you want to live your life stressed-out, unhealthy, in debt, or envious of other people who are fulfilling their dreams, you will end up miserable.

You must get fired up and determined by saying, "This is my final decision. I'm going to do it for me!" Behaviors play a major role here. We can either decide to act like mature adults or complain every time we don't get what we want, just like my six-year-old. I'm always amazed when I'm coaching adults and they say that they're so upset at someone—or better yet, mad at God—for missed opportunities. The formula for lasting success is "Better, not bitter." Imagine if you achieved what you desired but you were angry at the world. Your wealth would be plentiful, but your life would be miserable. Don't let people make you bitter; you work on being better, one action at a time! Remember that for every problem, there is a solution based on action. Here are some examples of this:

Problem: "My doctor told me that my heart needs to be strengthened, but I am a coffee addict and I love junk food.

He said I need to cut down on my caffeine and stop eating high fatty fried foods and start exercising!"

Action(s): Instead of referring to himself as a coffee addict and a fat lover, he could say, "My desire for coffee and fried foods is not going to control me. I am going to consume less caffeine and fried foods so that my heart will be stronger." When we make decisions, we must address the *why* behind the *how*. If we don't tell ourselves *why* we need to make changes, then *how* we're going to do it is twice as hard. The *why* motivates; the *how* validates.

In this particular case, the man's doctor told him that by limiting his high-fat food consumption and start exercising, he would strengthen his heart. That's the *why*. The *how* can be accomplished in numerous ways. For instance, this man could start by having one less cup of coffee at home before starting his workday. Or if that's too challenging, he could make his coffee at home a little weaker from now on. Then, on the way to work, he could buy a smaller size than he usually does; a medium instead of a large, for instance, or a small instead of a medium. Then at work, he could switch to decaf for that last cup of the morning. Any one of these very simple actions would help decrease his caffeine consumption.

Problem: "My boss won't promote me until I prove to her that I can excel at my job."

Action(s): The key to succeeding at work is to focus on one accomplishment at a time. Where, specifically, are you failing at work? Let's start there. If you're not getting to work on time, set your alarm fifteen minutes earlier every morning to make sure this simple error is corrected. If your boss thinks that your daily paperwork is sloppy, stay for a half hour after work every day until it's neat. If your interpersonal office skills are lacking, take action to correct this by working with a career coach, mentor, or counselor until you are more socially adept. You don't need a complete work overhaul; you just need to isolate the few areas in which you need to improve and then actively set about improving them, one action at a time. These small decisions will reap big rewards, because your boss will recognize that you value your job and her input.

Problem: "My spouse doesn't trust me. I need to show her I've changed my ways."

Action(s): Sometimes it's as important to *not* act as it is to act. By this I mean that if your actions are getting you into trouble, you need to take specific actions to *not* act in certain ways. For instance, let's say that your Thursday night out with the guys gets you into trouble with your wife every week. Maybe skip guys' night out next week and see how it goes. I'm not saying to change who you are if hanging out with the guys doesn't lead to trouble, but compromise *is* an action, and when you're in the doghouse, you need to take specific, corrective actions to get out. Maybe texting a certain female employee from your office about work projects at all hours of the day or night is making your wife feel threatened, jealous, or anxious. Take action to curb how often you text this coworker; set "office hours" on your phone and put some limits on your phone. Each, any, or all of these various actions can be taken gradually, day by day, to help build trust in your marriage.

See how simple this is? You must make a decision, alter your behavior, and then stick with it. If you're not that disciplined, enlist the help of someone who has healthy habits, like a friend, family member, or coach like me, or even join an online community of people with the same cause. Then instead of thinking about how difficult the task at hand will be, focus on the tremendous benefits you will gain from your actions. Stop repeating the problem and speak the solution: Then act on it!

Your actions will benefit every area of your life. Don't just take it from me. You count the cost of your actions. I call this the pain-gain threshold. It may be painful for you to deprive yourself of certain foods and start to exercise, but the gain is astronomical! You will:

• Lose body fat

- Improve circulation
- Increase cognitive reaction
- Move faster
- Feel better
- Breathe easier
- Be more confident
- Live longer
- Look better
- Decrease risk factors

If you get a 10 percent raise, you will:

- Have more to give to others (talk about joy!)
- Provide your family with more income
- Be able to save more for a rainy day
- Have more self-confidence at work
- Experience less work-related anxiety
- Pay off your debt
- Go shopping

If you improve your marriage, you will:

- Be happier and love life (trust me)
- Rekindle the romance
- Empower stability

- Have less relationship-centered anxiety
- Be more competent in your other relationships
- Look forward to going home
- Share more with your partner

The common denominator in all three of the above scenarios is *action*. Action is positively, absolutely, addictively addictive! The more you act, the more you want to act. The more you change, the more you want change. And if you can change just one thing, if you can act on one vital change agent and successfully complete it, you will prove to yourself that it's possible, which will make you desire more change— and more change and more change.

Like a ripple effect, changing just one area of your life will help you change others. For instance, let's say that you do manage to start exercising. It might not sound that momentous in black-and-white, but have you tried? Starting to exercise is tough, but if you succeed, it will give you the confidence to realize that such actions are repeatable. Maybe you've tried to start a workout regimen but never thought you'd succeed. Getting to the gym will give you the power to believe you can succeed in other areas as well, such as your job performance, marriage, other relationships, and finances. Succeeding in one area leads to succeeding in others, but you'll only feel that satisfaction—and potential— if you act now to succeed later.

All change requires action. And action gets results that reverberate throughout your entire life. A simple exercise like a short daily walk in the park will instantly spike your metabolism, not to mention decrease your biological aging by almost *ten* years! Curbing your spending by not acting on shopping whims will benefit you financially. Taking a 30-second break and thinking before speaking while in the midst of an argument with your spouse will help your marriage. Making a decision to get to work on time every day will translate into dependability in your boss's eyes.

When you put positive actions into play, change happens, and trust me, it happens fast. Remember that thoughts give rise to words and words give rise to actions, so be sure that your thoughts are positive and life-giving, and your actions will follow suit.

THE 30-SECOND THINKER:

"When I can't change *what* I'm looking at, I can change *the way* I'm looking at it."

MOTIVATE YOURSELF TO ACT

When we're working on motivating ourselves to act, we have to keep the long-term benefits in view. We are such an instant-gratification society that we'd never see an article with the title, "You Can Lose Fifty Pounds, but It's Going to Take You About Five Years, Lots of Self-Control, and Major Perseverance." Would you want to read that article? Probably not. We need to have a positive end in view when we're applying the 30-Second Solution to our lives. We have to think, "I can change that negative thought to a positive one in less than 30 seconds," or "I can take a 30-second break in the middle of this argument before responding," or "It will only take me 30 seconds to drive by the doughnut shop." All of these 30-second actions add up to a more positive, healthier, and stronger you. That's why keeping the long-term cumulative effects of these decisions in view will help you succeed.

There was a study done in the 1960s by Michael Mischel, a Stanford University psychology researcher, which showed how self-discipline is linked to success. The study began with a group of four-year-old kids. Mischel offered child one marshmallow each and told them if they could wait to eat the marshmallow until he returned twenty minutes later, they could have two marshmallows instead of one. He then left the one marshmallow out in full view and left the room. When he came back twenty minutes later, as expected, some children had gobbled up the marshmallow, some had waited for a while but then ate the marshmallow, and about a third of them had decided to wait and receive two marshmallows.

Fourteen years later, he followed up with the study participants (upon their high school graduations) and found substantial differences between the two groups in terms of wealth, overall happiness in life, and success. The children who delayed gratification were more positive when faced with difficulties, were more self-motivated, and had achieved their long-term goals with better success. The children who chose one marshmallow were more indecisive, less self-confident, and more troubled in general. The one-marshmallow students had SAT scores that were lower than the two-marshmallow students.

Which kind of person are you? Are you able to resist the marshmallows in your daily life? Intuitively, as an adult, you know that having self-control and waiting before you act rashly will bring you better results than giving in. But this study proves that making the right choices—however small—will, over time, make you more successful in the long run. You have the power to make changes, even very small changes that over time will add up to big results.

A client of mine epitomized this example. Paul had graduated from a liberal arts college with mediocre grades and was struggling to find what he wanted to do with his career. He was very impulsive and had trouble making decisions and committing, in both his personal and professional life.

He told me, "Yeah, I definitely would have been one of the one-marshmallow kids. In college, if I wanted the latest gadget or a new watch, I would go buy it on credit. If I wanted to go on a road trip, I'd do it. My roommate was the opposite. He definitely would have held out for the second marshmallow. He saved his money, studied more, and did much better academically than I did." I worked with Paul to use the 30-Second Solution whenever he wavered in his decision making or wanted to give in to his impulsive spending. Within six months, he has made significant strides. He landed a job in sales that he enjoyed and suited his nature, and he paid down his debts and started a savings plan. He explained, "While I couldn't change who I was, I did change my day-to-day actions one at a time." Paul made the decision to stop being a "one-marshmallow kid." It's a daily battle, but he is winning—one action at a time. While he may not be 100 percent successful all the time, his overall success is cumulative. If he can win the battle even 80 percent of the time, his life will be moving in a positive direction instead of a negative one.

DON'T JUST STARE UP THE STAIRS—
STEP UP THE STAIRS!

It's not enough to just stare up the stairs; you've got to step up the stairs. To get to the next level of life—physically, financially, emotionally, mentally, and spiritually—you're going to have to step up the stairs. In other words, thought is not enough; you have to act on what you know.

All movements have one thing in common: action. Movements move! It's time for you to take action now on that dream of yours. After all, you are not getting any younger, and time is the greatest commodity we have. You can never replace yesterday—or even the last five minutes. They're gone. What you have is *now* and the next 30 seconds. This is also important in fulfilling your personal desires, not just your career or your relationships and health. I remember telling one of my clients that he was not getting any younger, and if he was going to buy the car of his dreams, he'd better do it now! I told him to at least send away for all the brochures and specs on the car. He was in a place financially where he could pay cash for it, and his immediate action was not the purchase of the car but the information-gathering phase. In 30 seconds he placed the call, and in sixty days he had realized his goal of obtaining the car.

BUSYWORK VERSUS PURPOSEFUL ACTION

Many of you will say that your life is full of action; that you act all day long, moving here, going there—to work to the gym to a party, socializing with friends, bustling the kids here and there. Again, most of the "action" we commit in life is busywork. We think just because we're busy, active, and maybe even fit that we're acting on our purpose, power, and passion. Folks, we're not; we're not even close! I'm talking about the kind of action that is done with your dreams in mind, not just the day-to-day going-through-the motions kind of action.

For example, healthy action constitutes a way of living, not just a way of looking. It's not about how pretty you look on the outside, but how fit you are on the inside. It's not about your material success. I want to make this crystal clear: *you are more than what you are worth on paper.* The right action plan is found in understanding that even if you're not where you want to be—physically, financially, mentally, emotionally, or spiritually—the minute you start acting toward your goals, you are one step closer to achieving them.

It starts with belief. You have to believe you can do this! There will be setbacks, obstacles, and detours, but every time you face one, know that you have the ability to overcome it. That's action! Facing them! Maybe you're not exactly right for this job or that, but you have the ability to succeed if only given the chance. Say to yourself: *I may not have what I want right now, but I can become it; I'm going to get fit for this. I am going to do the right things in life to take the right action steps to get the life I want.*

What will it take to get the job of your dreams? Knowledge (of what the company needs for entry-level positions) combined with action (of what you need to do to get those skills). What will it take to get the body of your dreams? Knowledge (about how to eat, move, and live right), combined with action (eating, moving, and living right). What will it take to get the spouse of your dreams? Knowledge (about how to treat someone with respect, courtesy, and kindness), combined with action (being more respectful, courteous, and kind).

What does your heart say? When you have true knowledge of your goals and aspirations, when you believe in yourself, you never have trouble answering that question, because your heart will lead you to power, and power will lead to purpose, and purpose will lead to action. *The most powerful thing you could ever do for yourself and the world is to find out what you are created to do*—and do it!

I meet so many who are just going through the motions of life. It's time to go for your dreams! It takes guts. In order to win this game called life, you need focus, determination, and action.

ACTION BEATS ANALYSIS PARALYSIS

I'll never forget the phone call that I received years ago from a man who had inherited stock upwards of $30 million. He was about thirty-three when he called me, but around twenty-five at the time of his inheritance. The problem was that his inheritance gave him a lot more money in the financial bank than he had in what I call the life bank! Thirty million dollars. His father was a very wealthy businessman who sold his company for billions of dollars. I had the privilege and honor of working with these individuals and also coaching both of them.

To make a long story short: The man who inherited the money did not inherit wisdom or fiscal responsibility, and as a result, he lost $29 million of it. He inherited $30 million; he lost $29 million! I often say that "Wealth without wisdom will not last."

When I met him, the damage was already done. But his mother was able to talk him into coaching to see if we could help him turn his heath and life around. As you can imagine, the stress of that kind of loss affected everything about him.

When he inherited the money, he was afraid. He didn't have faith in his own ability to find an advisor or to research the market. He was afraid to see if his stocks were falling so he just assumed that if they did fall that they would magically bounce back. They were going lower, and lower, and lower, and he never pulled the trigger. All of this time, he was afraid of losing the money, so he did nothing. He took no action. He was afraid of how to invest the money to recover any potential loss; so he did nothing instead of taking purposeful action, like doing research online or hiring a financial coach. The constant fear of losing the money made him feel stressed and paralyzed him.

In the beginning, when the portfolio was up, he and his wife were having daily conversations along the lines of, "Should we buy the chandeliers that are made of crystal from Spain or should we go down to the local department store and just buy a chandelier there?" These are not bad conversations to have around the dinner table, but they were educating themselves on the products, not the portfolio. So one day I said to this man, "Did you ever think about picking up a book on financial development or asking a financial advisor to help you?"

I reminded him that this was not the end of the world; that if he would allow it, this situation would build character of heart. In addition, I reminded him that he still had $1million dollars left, and that he needed to exercise gratitude because all of it was a gift. I told him he could find wise financial advisors to help him make sound decisions to build his wealth once again. I coached him out of defeatism.

If you don't know how to take action, invest in books, CDs, sermons, or continuing education. In other words, invest in yourself to learn the right actions to take or find a trusted advisor to help you. Don't be afraid to ask for help in making the right actions.

Don't wait until catastrophe hits; kill the paralysis by picking up the phone and asking for help. Life does not have a remote control; you need to get up and change the channel yourself. Change is a choice and you must be mature enough to change. If you do, I promise you, you will experience action and results like never before.

KNOWLEDGE ISN'T JUST POWER—IT'S ACTION!

A very powerful principle I live by is the proverb, "My people are destroyed for lack of knowledge, because they reject knowledge" (Hosea 4:6, KJV). To change your direction in life, you must alter your knowledge about the decisions that will get you there. For example, I'm astonished by how much information is available on how to become wealthy and on how to lose weight. Yet the fact remains, if you don't apply it, you deny it! By this I mean that you deny its ability to work in your life. You can be whatever you want to be. You can be rich, you can be poor. You can be whatever you want, but you have to *know* what you want before you can be it. That's why knowledge is so powerful; it gives you the freedom to act while moving you in the right direction.

But more often than not, the people I coach are basically destroyed for a lack of knowledge or like the $30-million man subject to what is called "rejected knowledge." People with this mind-set know what they should do and choose not to do it. This is what contributes to defeatism rather than preparedness. Be prepared as best you can. Take the necessary action to cover your bases in whatever goal you are trying to achieve.

Ignorance comes from the word *ignore*. It happens when you consciously ignore something you know you should learn.

Robert Kiyosaki, author of Rich Dad, Poor Dad

ACTION IS TENACITY BACKED BY A SKILL SET

Most CEOs and entrepreneurs know they have to be bold but educated. In today's world people often want something for nothing. We all feel that way from time to time. Once you realize that great success comes with a great price, your attitude changes. Tenacity (the action of persevering) backed by humility (knowing that we don't know everything) ensures tremendous results no matter what field we're in, because it builds a regard for human life within the core of our souls. It consciously resists the "I will run you over" mentality that our fast-paced, success-oriented culture often fosters. I am not saying that anyone should be a pushover; it's a much deeper action than that.

The key to achieving your dreams is to be knowledgeable about what you are doing and tenacious in getting there, all while allowing humility to season you so that you're not misconstrued as a greedy capitalist who will do anything, at any cost, to get what you want. Most people recognize the real deal when they see it.

Successful people are willing to do things that most people will never do. They have a spirit of willingness that everyone wants but that most are unwilling to pay for. These people have a genuine desire to respect others regardless of their station in life. They know they have something to learn from the corporate president *and* the hot dog vendor.

PATIENCE ISN'T JUST A VIRTUE, IT'S AN ACTION

Sometimes the best way to "act" is not to act at all. In fact, cultivating patience can be a very powerful spiritual action.

The following story is a good illustration. At an intersection by our home, traffic was completely backed up. A man in his work truck decided to drive into the oncoming traffic and speed around all the other cars in his lane. He didn't pause for 30 seconds to think about how his actions would affect others (and himself). Instead, he impulsively decided to race around traffic and run a red light. At the same time, a young father was returning home on his bike after having dropped his daughter off at school. The man driving the work truck rushed through the intersection, killing the young father on impact.

In this case, just a 30-second pause—and *not* acting—could have saved the young father's life and prevented three thirty-year jail sentences for the driver. The driver's action affected so many others besides himself, his family, and his friends—the deceased dad, his precious wife, his child, his parents, extended family members, and friends—all because he acted impulsively instead of waiting. In this particular case, *not* acting would have been the most powerful action.

ACTION IS THE FINAL KEY TO SUCCESS

The missing ingredient in most would-be success stories is, quite simply, action. You can't sit in your room the rest of your life thinking yourself into success; you can't stand in front of the mirror for the rest of the year speaking yourself into success. Decisions and ideas are powerless unless we act on them. To be successful—to truly reach your goals and accomplish your plans—you must act. The good news is that there is no time like the present. The even better news is that you now have all three tools to succeed in applying the *30-Second Solution* to all areas of your life: positive thinking, precise speaking, and purposeful acting.

 While some coaches would push you to move, in many cases, your action is to not move but to rethink your move. Choosing to "respond" versus "re-act" is often the best solution. In other cases, if you find yourself procrastinating, you need to act. Type a letter, send yourself a text message, or make that phone call. All constitute action, yet in each situation, be mindful, gain wisdom from people you trust, go inward before you go outward, and act according to truth.

CHAPTER 5:

BIG Method—BIG Movement— BIG RETURN!

I love looking at methodological approaches to life, because that's what works for me. But everyone has different methods for reaching the same end. Ask my wife how she wants the kitchen to look, and she has her own method for achieving a certain look and cleaning it a certain way. When you're driving, you observe signposts at every corner and intersection because there is a method in place called the U.S. road systems that will get you where you need to go. When you begin working for a company, it usually provides an employee handbook that includes the methods the company expects its employees to use to ensure that everyone is on the same page about what is expected.

When you employ a method of positive change in your life, it doesn't change just one thing but creates an entire movement. *Webster's* dictionary describes a movement as "a series of organized activities [actions] working toward an objective; *also*: an organized effort to promote or attain an end (the civil rights *movement*)." As you initiate change in one area of your life through positive action, you often discover that other areas of your life change for the better as well. When you begin to reap the rewards of positive thinking, precise speaking, and purposeful action in your own life, it also makes an impact on the lives of people around you. By learning how to apply the 30-Second Solution to how you think, speak, and act, you have a simple, proven way to begin pursuing the life you've always wanted, or, as I call it, living out loud!

RUTS AND ROADBLOCKS

I wouldn't be a very good encourager if I left out the fact that even good change can cause stress in your life. Anyone who has ever welcomed a new baby into the family knows that with the great blessing of that new life also comes sleepless nights, dirty diapers, and emotional and financial stress.

It takes a time of adjustment for everyone. As you make positive changes in your life, you will inevitably run into some
roadblocks and ruts along the way, some from within and
some from outside influences. These may include:

- Naysayers and negative people who do not support you
  (and don't be surprised if these people are among your
  friends and family)
- Fear of failing or depression
- Lack of motivation, apathy, or boredom

Let's consider a few of these roadblocks and ruts on the
list, beginning with negative people. There will always be
Negative Nellies in the world; some people just can't bear
the happiness and contentment of others. For some reason, when we start making positive changes in our lives,
we encounter resistance—and sometimes from our closest
friends and family. Often the impetus behind this lack of
support is jealousy. These people see that we're motivated
and committed to change, and it threatens them. If we cut
back on fattening and sugary foods, who will they indulge
with? If we quit smoking, whom will join them behind the
garage for a cigarette break? You need to stand strong with
your newfound knowledge and lovingly tell them that they're
free to join you for a smoothie at the local health-food store

or a cup of coffee at the local (nonsmoking) coffee shop. Who knows? Maybe they'll see how much happier you are and want to join you on this new quest. But if they never support you, you're strong enough to do it without them. Seek out support groups for your interests, and you'll always be able to find like-minded people who share your desire for change and optimism.

Fear of failing is another roadblock that you may encounter. Just remember what Eleanor Roosevelt said: "We gain strength, and courage, and confidence by each experience in which we really stop to look fear in the face . . . we must do that which we think we cannot." You will not fail! The beauty of the 30-Second Solution is that every second is a new beginning. If you veer off the path momentarily, regardless of your goal, get up and resolve to stay on the path. Here's the greatest truth: if we don't quit, we win! Remember my promise to you in the introduction of this book? I promised you that if you embrace the 30-Second Solution and apply it to the way you think, speak, and act, you will see results. I made that promise in good faith, because I believe in you!

Concerning depression, you cannot be a healthy example until you yourself are healed, and by healing, I am not referring to just the physical realm, but also to the emotional, mental, and spiritual ones. At some point, you may stop believing in your values and your purpose in life, and everything erodes from there. You might be saying, "I don't believe in me; I'm very introverted, no one loves me." Or you may be struggling with the changes in physical appearance that often accompany aging. If you have always felt valued by the beauty of your physical appearance and gravity is setting in on you, you need to come to a new place of acceptance about that. You need to look at the root of your fears and insecurities about the aging process and find a way to embrace your changing physique. If you have put too much emphasis on outer appearance, maybe you need to adjust that value in your life and realize that gaining wisdom along with a few pounds and wrinkles is worth the price. Whatever is causing your depression, if you feel that your problems are beyond your ability to solve them alone, be sure to seek out friends, mentors, life coaches, or therapists who can help.

Now let's consider the ruts: lack of motivation, apathy, and boredom. One of the definitions of *rut* is "a monotonous routine." If you're unmotivated and find yourself feeling apathetic and bored, it likely means that you need to switch your routines. If you've been using the same type of exercise for a long time, this would be a good time to start something new. If you're tired of swimming, start a kickboxing class. If you've lost interest in working out at the gym, talk your partner, a family member, or a friend into taking square-dancing or ballroom-dancing lessons with you. With all the choices we have for exercising today, if we're suffering from boredom, we're definitely suffering from a lack of imagination.

Nearly every small town in America offers adult education courses. Maybe it's time for you to learn how to speak Spanish or Chinese, cook Greek or Thai food, or learn how to belly dance. Go to the library or your local bookstore and select several books on subjects that you've always found interesting. Read a motivational book by one of the many excellent life coaches. You can be the architect of your brain by learning something new and blazing new neural pathways. The world is your oyster!

HANDLING STRESS BEFORE IT HANDLES YOU

According to recent Gallup polls, many Americans report that the state of the economy has caused stress in their lives. High unemployment rates and job cuts have caused concerns about the future. One study found that 62 percent of Americans believe economic conditions are getting worse, while 47 percent described current economic conditions as poor (a year earlier, 44 percent gave economic conditions a poor rating). Other concerns of Americans noted on the Gallup website include continued unrest in the Middle East, the war in Libya, and ongoing catastrophes in Japan due to the March 2011 earthquake and tsunami. Closer to home, there are real anxieties about unemployment, the high price of gas and food, and the budget battles in the government.[14]

A study by the Principal Financial Group found that 75 percent of American workers and retirees are very concerned about their financial future. One-third of those asked said stress levels about their financial situation are much higher now than they were a year ago.[15]

With all the uncertainty in the world today, both at home and abroad, stress levels are definitely high. Bodies that are under stress respond by releasing stress hormones, such as cortisol and adrenaline. These hormones cause increases in blood pressure, blood glucose levels, and heart rate, which can then cause high blood pressure, heart disease, depression, and other health problems. When cortisol levels remain high for too long, they can affect your brain by diminishing your decision-making process, among other effects. Since stress is inevitable in our world, it's very important that we have what experts call a stress-management system in place.[16] You can practice stress-relieving techniques such as exercise and meditation at home or in a class. Some areas offer free stress-reduction classes, so be sure to check your community information boards (online or at the library) to see what's available where you live. Breathing exercises are very effective in helping relieve stress, as are aromatherapy, gardening, playing and listening to music, and sex (for those who are married and want to develop a better brain look it up on the web!). Whatever stress reliever you incorporate into your life, make it part of your daily routine. Don't wait until your stress load is so heavy it starts affecting your health; be preemptive and begin now. Then when the stressful times come—and they will—you'll already have something in place to counter them.

THE POWER OF BELIEF

I want you to truly believe that you can, will, and absolutely should succeed. Belief is so important. As a coach, I believe that all human beings have much more potential inside them than they think they have.

I believe that you are uniquely made, and you need to receive this message into your spirit and heart. The seeds of greatness are in you. Do you realize that the first fight in your life was the fight to be born? And you made it! What makes you think you will fail now? You were meant to live on earth at this particular time in history.

Whose voice in your life keeps telling you that you can't go bigger? Who's the name caller in your life? You're not six anymore; you don't need to believe the names you're called or the labels people put on you. In fact, there's only one thing you need to believe, and that's what *you* believe, not what they believe. You're not called to please people; you're called to love them.

I learned a long time ago to avoid people-pleasing, and I told Tia, "You and I are not going to get into people-pleasing. I cannot afford for my mind to be so consumed by what others think about what I'm wearing, how I'm driving, what job I have, how I raise my children, where I go, and what I do."

We decided to make a behavioral change in our belief system and delete people-pleasing from our lives and our sphere of influence. Imagine if Jesus or Gandhi or Mother Teresa had really cared what people thought them. Imagine if past presidents were moved by the things people thought about them. They didn't have time to agonize about what people thought of them and their decisions, because they had a job to do. And this is the perspective you need to adopt in your own life. You have to get to the point where your belief system is such that it really doesn't matter what others think about you, because your self-belief is more important than what they believe about you.

As for me, I know my belief system and who I am. When

the door closes at night and I kneel before my bedside, lay my head on my pillow, and take a spiritual inventory at the end of the day, I know who I am because of the way I think, speak, and act, and I don't need to make any apologies for it.

As you begin to address the critical areas of your life and how to achieve success in them, you have to believe that you can change. It's time to believe in your own personal metamorphosis, starting right now.

HOW TO DEFINE YOUR GOALS
AND LIFE VISION

Did you know that in the American marketplace today, 70 percent of those who leave their jobs do so because they do not feel valued? Don't you want others to accept you for who you are and show you through their actions that you matter?

A friend of mine, whom I'll call Scout, wanted to be a record producer. He loved music; he lived music. He'd grown up spending every week's allowance on the latest cassette tapes, then CDs, and then MP3 downloads. He still spent every waking moment, to say nothing of his income, on music.

Scout had a day job that he hated; he constantly complained about working at the insurance company, yet rather than do anything about saving up to start his own record label or even stashing away six months of "transition money" to hold him over while he looked for work in the record industry, he spent all his time, energy, and money on music.

I know Scout's thoughts were in the right place because music was his soul. And he talked the talk, but he simply couldn't walk the walk. In other words, though his mind and his mouth were geared toward working in music, his actions said otherwise, because he never did anything concrete to reach his goals.

If humility is the key to a successful relationship, then goals are the key to a successful career. According to Dan Zadra, author of the book *5: Where Will You Be Five Years from Today?*, people who regularly write down their goals earn nine times as much over their lifetimes as people who don't, and yet a whopping 80 percent of Americans say they don't have goals! Sixteen percent do have goals, but they don't write them down. Less than 4 percent write down their goals, and less than 1 percent actually achieve them. I encourage you to take the time to write down your goals, visions, and plans for the future.

Purpose comes from your cause. Remember your cause? We talked about it in Chapter 1. I asked you to write down your cause then, and here's why: without a cause, you will find it difficult to articulate and follow your purpose. Before I devoted my life to helping others, I floundered from job to job, bed to bed, and bounced check to bounced check. I thought my purpose in life was to consume, take up space, and fulfill my needs at the expense of others. What a revelation it was when I discovered that my cause was to help others fulfill their dreams!

Suddenly—literally, overnight—my life had new meaning. I now had a purpose to pursue, an ultimate goal to achieve, and from then on, every motion was forward motion. The goal is to find your purpose, whatever that may be, and once you do, focus on it. Give it power with positive praise and optimistic mental imagery and words of life.

GOALS ARE STEPPING-STONES TO FULFILLING YOUR VISION

Goals are the stepping-stones that support your vision. You can also think of them as micro-bursts that generate the power you need to fulfill your purpose in life. I encourage you to formulate goals in three areas of your life:

- Personal (including health, finances, and spirituality)
- Family

• Business or corporate

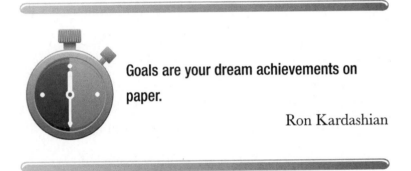

Goals are your dream achievements on paper.

Ron Kardashian

You can break these goals down into even smaller categories if it's more helpful. For instance, under "Personal," you
might want to include subcategories of goals, such as "Walk
three miles every morning before work," "Save 10 percent
of each paycheck," and "Spend one-half hour meditating
daily." I suggest you be as detailed as you can and then write
down one or two sentences explaining why you want to pursue each specific thing. This is addressing the *why* behind
your *how*: Why do you want to achieve this particular goal?
Here is an example from my life:

1. **Personal:** (a) Health: Exercise five days per week;
   weight train for three out of five of the days. I will do
   this because I want to be as fit as I can be so I will have

the energy I need to accomplish my goals. (b) Finances: Increase salary by X amount and give away X amount of money to charitable causes. The more money I make, the more I can give away! (c) Spiritual: Go to church every Sunday. Meditate every morning before first appointment of the day. Staying hooked-in spiritually fuels my life.

2. **Family:** Keep my date night with Tia on _____. Take time off this year to spend with my family. I will do this is because my first calling is to my wife and children; everything else is secondary.

3. **Business:** Expand viewing audiences. By February we will _____. By March we will _____. By April _____, and so on. Reaching wider audiences will help more people and keep our business alive and dynamic.

Of course, these are just a few examples. Your list of goals will be as unique as you are.

MAKE A VISION BOARD

One way to cement your purpose in your mind is to engage in the following exercise: create a "vision board" that includes pictures related to your purpose. Pull pictures of your dream life from magazines, websites, and so on: people, places to visit, material things, and other images that speak to your vision. I have had a vision board in my home for more than fifteen years, and it grows every couple of years (I'm actually living in the home I posted back then, which still amazes me). Really visualize your purpose, down to the clothes you'll wear, where it will take place, what time of day, and in what city, state, or country.

Besides using a vision board, every morning I wake up and visualize my day. I start with my studio, where open blinds let in the California sun and hardwood floors allow for freedom of motion. Then I picture the clients I'll have that day—what they look like, what I'll do with them, what we'll discuss, and how they'll look when I'm finished. I literally picture their smiles as a result of our sessions, and then I set about making those smiles a reality by following up my visualization exercise with words and action.

Here are four simple steps to bring your own purpose to life by visualizing it:

1. **Start with yourself.** Truly, it all starts with you. What do you dream of doing? What are you doing? What are you wearing? How are you feeling? Don't just pay lip service to these questions; really close your eyes and

imagine the answers as they spring to life right before your mind's eye!

2. **Next, envision where you are.** Is it in a forest? A garage? An office? A movie theater, red carpet, recording studio, or soundstage? The more details you can contribute to your mental vision, the more real it will feel, and it's all about the realism.

3. **Then, picture who you're with.** Is it a client? A customer? A boss, spouse, family member, friend, or coworker? Don't stop with a job title; picture what the people are wearing, how they've done their hair, what they say, and even how they say it.

4. **Finally, visualize what happens.** Really see yourself moving in your mind's eye. When I'm deep into my morning visualization exercise, I can actually hear the squeak of my tennis shoes on the wood flooring and feel the warmth of the sun on my hands! These detailed images help to make my mental exercise a reality.

Here are some great statements to help you focus on your purpose in a way that is real, meaningful, and powerful to you:

• Everything that was created was created with a purpose!
• My purpose has meaning, even if I haven't fulfilled it yet.

- I can share my purpose with anyone, at any time, because I "own" it.
- I don't have to readjust my purpose just because it's not popular, timely, or fashionable.
- My purpose may take time; I can't—and shouldn't—expect overnight results.

Acting with purpose doesn't take time or money; it simply takes commitment. And, trust me, when you find your purpose—and I sincerely pray you already have—you won't be able to wait to act on it! Until then, if you're still searching for your purpose, act toward your purpose. By that, I mean do things that foster more purpose in your life, including:

- Praying
- Taking courses that pique your interest
- Choosing jobs that feel right (deep within you)
- Going to seminars and workshops that help you better yourself
- Consorting with like-minded people who inspire you

DETERMINE YOUR MISSION

Outstanding people have one thing in common:
an absolute sense of mission.

Zig Ziglar

Before you can write your mission and vision statements, you must identify your cause. We spoke about having a cause and values in the beginning of the book. I have include this graphic illustration to remind you of how critical your cause is in shaping your values followed by your mission and vision for your life:

Why do you need a cause before you write your mission statement?
Because a mission is formulated around your cause, and your values
support the structure of your mission. For instance, since my cause in
life is to help others improve their lives,
my mission is "To empower extraordinary life."

In fact, that's my mission statement. This simple, one-sentence statement guides my life by always bringing my thoughts, words, and actions into focus. Mission statements are like mental reminders of what, exactly, we're trying to accomplish and fulfill. That's why nearly every successful company has a mission statement; it gives the employees a one-sentence attitude adjustment if they ever get off course.

Remember, this book is not about just surviving—it's about reviving your body, mind, and spirit! Creating a mission statement for yourself lets you focus and see your cause in such a way that it's always on your mind, or when it's out of mind, a simple refresher course of visualizing it can and will get you back on track.

What does a mission statement look like? Here are some examples of famous people's mission statements that worked—and worked well:

- Walt Disney: "My mission in life is to make people happy."
- Eric Schmidt, CEO of Google.com: "My mission is to collect all the world information and make it accessible to everyone."
- Bijan, a friend and famous clothing designer: "My mission is to design the finest clothing in the world."
- Phil Knight, founder of Nike: "My mission is to bring inspiration and innovation to every athlete in the world."

- My mission: "My mission is to empower others and organizations with an extraordinary life and company!"

See how these missions are simple, focused, and uncomplicated? They are one-sentence statements of power and purpose, simply said and easy to apply whenever one's attitude needs adjusting. So what is *your* mission? How can you put the cause you've already determined into powerful action in your life in a way that is meaningful to yourself and others? Answer the question in the space provided below before moving on, and remember:

1. Your mission statement should be no more than one sentence long.
2. A seven-year-old should be able to understand it. (My daughter is seven and is very clear about what her daddy does.)
3. Your mission is wrapped around your cause.
4. Your mission is made visible and concrete by your values.

What is your mission?

_____

_____

_____

_____

CRAFT YOUR VISION STATEMENT

Whatever you visualize will materialize— make no mistake about it.

Ron Kardashian

Your cause determines the mission you accept in life. Your mission is the practical application of your cause in your daily activities. Your vision is how you're going to achieve your mission. In other words, a vision statement is like your action plan for getting your mission done. For instance, how will I achieve my mission of empowering extraordinary life? I will follow my vision statement, a declaration of how I will hold myself accountable for achieving my mission. This is why it's so important to visualize your success!

Remember that you will become what you think about. If you're limiting your vision because you are only looking at the surface of your dreams, you need to dig deeper and dream bigger. When it comes to your vision statement, think *big* and allow your words and actions to follow suit.

Your vision statement has one purpose: to make your mission visible so that you can put an action plan in place to fulfill it. Once you craft your vision statement, you need to write it on paper and hang it up where you will see it clearly every day. You could put it in your office, on the bathroom mirror, on the fridge in the kitchen, or on your mobile device.

If you are the leader of a company and don't have your vision statement up on the wall, get it up there. Having your vision statement in a prominent position at the workplace changes the entire environment. Why? Because everyone who works there, from the CEO to the janitorial service, will be on the same page and will collectively pursue your vision for the company.

I saw this work firsthand when Tia and I got married. We made a vision statement for our marriage and put it up in a prominent place at home. The two of us began to pursue our marriage vision—and fast! When we saw how this kept us focused in our personal lives, we decided to apply it in our companies, from major tech companies to food and beverage companies, and it worked there as well. When we all have the same vision for the company, the power of agreement actively thrusts us forward. As CEOs and leaders, it gives us a platform to continually speak from, reiterating the vision until it becomes crystal clear within the hearts of our employees. Be passionate about speaking your vision, whether it's doing hair in a living room salon or running the Senate. Expressing your vision statement with clarity and stellar communication will keep you on the road to success.

When writing your vision statement, be as specific as you can be:

1. I will make sure I do this every week.
2. By this date I will have _____ fulfilled.
3. I will list specific goals to achieve my mission in life by addressing the *why* behind my *how*.

4. I will educate myself in the areas where I know
   I need development.

5. I will acquire the tools I need to fulfill my mission.

6. I will surround myself with experts so that I will get
   this done within a reasonable time frame.

Now it's time to write down your vision statement:

_____

_____

_____

_____

Now write down the *why* of your vision statement:
Why am I going to achieve this?

_____

_____

_____

_____

Now meld the two areas of mission and vision and you
have your Mission and Vision Statement (MVS) which is
supported by your cause and values. Now you have the *what*,
how, and *why* of what you're going to achieve in your life. So,

armed with your MVS, you become an MVP. (This is just a play on words, but I want you to understand that value is instilled with people who support it with a cause, a mission, and a vision, thus making you the most valuable person you can be.)

GIVE YOUR LIFE TO LIVE YOUR LIFE

Happiness is not so much in having as sharing. We make a living by what we get, but we make a life by what we give.

Norman McEwen

You have so much to live for. The very breath in your lungs is something noteworthy to appreciate. When my wife was diagnosed with asthma, it was so hard on our family. Today she has overcome it with good nutrition, stress-free living, and exercise (that I prescribed for her). All those years she wanted to exercise, but she just did not have the lung capacity to do so. Yet so many people fail to appreciate the God-given gift of breathing. Keeping an attitude of gratitude during the transitions of life is vital to staying happy. And that's precisely what she did!

During the years I was developing the 30-Second Solution we made a list of everything we could do in 30 seconds that could make us happy and even change our lives. We listed sayings we could speak silently or to each other, such as, "We have one another." or "We may not be where we want to be but at least we are working to get there," or "Let's give thanks for 30 seconds for each other!" It was very powerful.

I have given you a very powerful list at the end of this book of 30-second solutions to curb depression, anxiety, and even failure. Reaching for life's simplicities is a powerful force to empower change. And I'm speaking of change emotionally that will empower good actions. Each of us defines happiness in our own unique way. In fact, the reason we all seek happiness is that the feeling is so pleasant, so warm, so reaffirming, and so replenishing that we can't help but try to return there again and again The list, along with all the 30-second tools in this book, will keep you fine-tuned and getting stronger.

For me, happiness is my relationship with my Creator, a loving spouse, my beautiful children, safety and security, my career satisfaction, good food and good friends, and empowering others to be the best they can be. For you, happiness might mean success, achievement, money, romance, church, career—they're all okay. The fact is, happiness is different for everyone. So why do I include it as one of my basic essentials in life if it's so hard to define? Simple: we can't live without it. Sure, we might be able to *survive* without happiness. Food, water, clothing, and shelter might keep us physically alive, but to revive your life and truly live it—long and proud and out loud—I want you to pursue the kind of joy that produces a perpetual state of happiness.

ACT JOYFULLY: IT ALL BEGINS (AND ENDS) IN THE BRAIN

More than almost any other reality, joy begins and ends in the brain. The problem is, very few of us truly, genuinely, deep down in our souls believe that we are supposed to be happy. It's true! Too often we think that the minute something goes "right" in our life, it's destined to go "wrong" just as quickly. Clients often say to me, "Ron, I'm too happy right now; I'm afraid of what's going to happen when the other shoe drops!" I say, "Let it!" Seriously, maybe the other shoe is a big clown foot that will bring you twice as much happiness as the first! To help you overcome the negative messages that unnecessarily accompany your happiest thoughts, here are some 30-second statements to meditate on:

- Joy is an inward working of my heart. I am joyful for life and that brings happiness.
- Being happy today doesn't necessarily mean I'll be unhappy tomorrow.

- There is nothing wrong with being happy.
- I deserve to be happy; all people do.
- I created this happiness, so now I get to enjoy it.
- Happiness is awesome when I can share it with others.
- Happiness stems from joy, and joy is healthy for my body. I choose to think about things that bring me joy. (Breath in my lungs, my kids, my family, my work, my hobbies, places I've visited, etc., bring me joy)
- Being happy is my choice and I choose to be joyful.

SPEAK HAPPINESS

Thinking happy thoughts is relatively simple, but speaking happiness into existence becomes much more challenging given our hang-ups about just simply "being" happy. Seriously, how many times have you avoided verbalizing a positive occurrence in your life because you don't want to jinx it? But stop with the fear. Speak your joy loud and clear. What you continue to speak will eventually manifest in your life— not just in the moment but over time.

My colleague Sheila just received a publishing contract from a major publisher. She is so excited, but she refuses to talk about it: not out loud, not on Facebook with an announcement to her friends, not even via a 140-character tweet!

Now, I know other people who loudly proclaim every time they write a legible sentence, let alone get a book published, but Sheila is convinced that if she opens her mouth and tells the world how happy she is, to say nothing of what she's happy about, then sudden doom, despair, and tragedy will somehow befall her. The other day I asked her when she would formally announce the book's publication. She said, "When I see it for myself, sitting on the bookshelf in a bookstore!"

I admire her self-control, but I think she's missing out on experiencing happiness along the path to publication. Do you know how long it takes for a book to be published? Conservatively speaking, anywhere from nine to sixteen months! So rather than spend most of a year, or more than a year, celebrating, Sheila is literally putting her happiness on hold. After all that time she spends worrying and agonizing over the potential problems that might arise prior to publication, I wonder if she'll ever really be genuinely happy when the book actually comes out.

Don't be like Sheila; enjoy your happiness, embrace it, celebrate it—*now*! How? Through words. Speak your happiness and dreams into existence. Before I got my publishing contract, I said to my wife and my kids, "Guess what, guys? Daddy is going to get my second book published. Isn't that wonderful?" They all shouted, "Yeah!" Talk about joy! Speaking your happiness to the right people creates a spiritual force to move in your favor. Words carry weight. They are alive and they have life in them. To make your happiness real, to invite it in when you're down, to heighten it when you're up, to make a mediocre day happy, and a happy day happier. Begin using more words of expectation in your daily speech patterns. Think of your words like containers. You can either fill them with fear, apprehension, and anger or choose to fill them with faith and joy. I am convinced that my words are creating my destiny. Try filling your speech with these words of happiness as a start:

- Yes!
- I believe.
- Relief!
- Delight!
- I Am.
- I can!
- Celebrate!
- Now!
- Today!
- Hallelujah!

ACTIONS THAT PROMOTE HAPPINESS

Earlier in this chapter I shared some of the Kardashian family values and how they guide us to purposeful action in every area of our lives. As I coach CEOs and people with both small and big dreams all over the world, I find they all share one thing in common: faith. That belief activates their actions. And your faith will activate your actions, too. Have faith, and 30 seconds is all you need to be increasingly happier.

For starters, you can smile! It's that simple. It doesn't even take 30 seconds. Smiling can lift your spirits. A study conducted by the British Dental Health Foundation showed the act of smiling to "dramatically improve one's mood."[17] Smiling has also been shown to improve the moods of others (i.e., making others happy) and relieve stress, which naturally makes you feel happier. And did you know that it requires less facial muscles to smile than it does to frown? It's true!

Also, the practice of smiling enacts the law of reciprocity. To *reciprocate* means to make a return for something given. In other words, when you smile others will return your smile with a smile, Reciprocity affects what you give yourself (a smile), your cause, your business, and your relationships and what you do unto others. The ancient saying is true: "Do unto others as you would have them do unto you." Or "It all comes back to you." Some people call it karma. The law of reciprocity is one of my most powerful coaching tools. Over time, understanding this universal law brings tremendous inherent happiness. It is essential to live the law of reciprocity as you work on your own 30-second solutions.

The law of reciprocity tell us:

- Gratitude yields thankfulness
- Our attitude toward life determines life's attitude toward us.
- What you truly believe will show in your behaviors.
- How you think is how you will speak.
- What you give is what you get.
- What you sow is what you will reap.
- And so on.

Reciprocity works in every dimension of one's life. The number-one way to stop the flow of happiness in your life is to do things to others that you would not want done to you. The same principle applies to your business dealings: don't slander and speaking badly about your organization or the people in it. The law of reciprocity will take you on a downward spiral and leave you lonely.

When the book *The Secret* hit worldwide, my family and I had been living the law of reciprocity for years. But I reminded all my clients that not only does the law work for the good in life, it also works for the bad. When your actions are not for the betterment of others, reciprocity still works. Bad actions breed negativity. If other people talk negatively that does not mean you have to talk back! Taking 30 seconds to give positive life to the situation will alter your sphere of influence and create a forum for you to speak positively with generosity and reap a happy life, business, and countenance.

Acting with reciprocity is key to achieving your own personal goals and internal happiness. When you live by the law of reciprocity, happiness and joy are inevitable. Tia and I live the law of reciprocity everywhere we go. We live with an understanding that our thoughts, words, and actions plant seeds. And seeds grow to produce results. We plant seeds of positivity and love so we can reap positivity and love.

The same principle applies to work. When you know you're doing the best of your ability and your business dealings are from a pure intention, you can expect good and big things to happen. It's a law. Reciprocity leads to networking in business, to healthy social interactions in relationships, to solid investments in finances, and to overall good vibes in just about everything else! Allow good things to flow into your life by making honest and pure decisions that will bring happiness to others and happiness to your life. It only takes 30 seconds to stop yourself from speaking badly about another person, and it only takes 30 seconds to do the right thing every time. In the end, you will be richer and healthier and a whole lot happier.

Other actions that can increase the amount of happiness in your day include:

- Exercise reaps health.
- Meditation reaps relaxation.
- Prayer reaps answers.
- Laughter reaps health and relief.
- Talking to positive people who have your best interest in mind yields power.
- Being friendly yields friendships and love.

All of us have heard the saying "Actions speak louder than words." But as we have learned throughout this book, while actions may speak louder than words, all actions originate from words, and words begin with thoughts. Now that you know the simplicity, yet effectiveness, of the 30-Second Solution, to think positively, speak precisely, and act purposefully in all areas of life—including physically, financially, emotionally, mentally, and spiritually—you have the power to change your life. The next 30 seconds begin . . . now! Seconds do matter.

A simple change today will bring a dramatic change tomorrow.

Ron Kardashian

Things Everyone Can Do in 30 Seconds!

- Reply with a warm "thank you."
- Say "I love you" to your loved one.
- Commit to exercise.
- Move.
- Show respect.
- Suck your stomach in.
- Hold your breath.
- Flex any muscle.
- Read a food label.
- Say "no" to a food you know is not good for you.
- Do the right thing, even if it hurts.
- Pass on dessert.
- Be mature.
- Help someone onto an airplane.
- Forgive.

- Practice humility.
- Make a phone call and tell someone "I'm sorry."
- Let go.
- Pray.
- Express gratitude. Compose a thank-you letter.
- Give a small smile to someone with a big frown.
- Ask someone to forgive you.
- Refrain from yelling at your spouse.
- Write "I love you" on a sticky note.
- Love the loveless.
- Get a cup of water for someone.
- Practice self-control.
- Refrain from releasing your anger in public.
- Hold your tongue from bashing someone you know deserves it.
- Speak a kind word.
- Send a gift to someone who did a favor for you.
- Maintain composure. Stay calm when your child makes a mistake.
- Go to the gym.
- Feed a homeless person.
- Sing a song.
- Brush your little girl's hair.
- Hold your little boy.

- Drink a glass of spring water.
- Stop. Take a breath and thank God for your
  lungs and your life.
- Dream about what would be your ultimate life.
- Choose to honor someone.
- Choose not to compromise.
- Kiss.
- Hug.
- Be giving. Make a donation to a church or
  an organization.
- Pledge to give something to someone less fortunate.
- Refrain from getting angry when someone
  does you wrong.
- Write down a goal.
- Pray for a nation.
- Pray for a stranger.
- Think about another rather than yourself.
- Love extravagantly.
- Refuse to be reactionary.
- And the list goes on and on . . .

I know you have what it takes. It only takes 30 seconds.

All my love and prayers,

Coach Ron

Bonus Section:
The 30-Second
CEO Within You

Everyone in life is a CEO. You are the chief executive officer of your own mind and body. You can achieve a massive turnaround in your health and life in 30 seconds as you meditate on this truth. A positive mind-set will give you the ability to think BIG! And so it has been for most of the CEOs I have had the privilege of meeting and coaching. They are BIG thinkers and they yield BIG results. However, some CEOs are among the unhealthiest people I have ever met! Success is not just net worth but self-worth. You are your greatest investment. Without you—there is no CEO.

A friend of mine received an eight-figure funding for his company. I was amazed that at such a young age he was allotted such a vast sum of money. You'd think he would be on easy street! However, as the year went on, he put anything he wanted in his mouth, he got heavier, his marriage began to suffer, and he was always sick.

Men and woman all over the country focus so much attention on building their businesses that they stop caring for themselves completely. I call it the "Net-Worth/Self-Worth Syndrome." What good will you be to your company, to say nothing of your family and friends, if you eat your way to excess pounds and add endless anxiety from stress that creates the perfect storm for a heart attack before you're sixty?

Some of you might be saying to yourself, "I'll do whatever it takes to succeed! Everyone needs to sacrifice." I understand you. Believe me, my life is a compromise every day built on a variety of sacrifices. However, there are hundreds of CEOs who *do* start successful companies and don't end up putting on extra weight or placing their families in second place.

Remember, gaining too much weight can be fatal. Weighing 30 percent above your ideal puts you at risk for twenty-six diseases, twelve of which are fatal. While money is an asset, extra weight is definitely *not* something you want to accumulate. At the end of the day, a company is never more important than you and your health.

And yet, almost every day, we put business before health; success before our own well-being. Remember my young eight-figure friend who was letting his health go? I was shocked by how this gentleman would never allow anything to corrupt his business. If a virus would invade the company's software, he would put a whole team on the problem; if that didn't work, he himself—the boss—would stay up all night finding a solution. However, he failed to focus on the solution when it came to fighting for his marriage or winning the battle of the bulge.

Consider one of the most successful organizations in the world, the United States armed forces, which instills in its "CEOs," or leaders, the importance of physical fitness and training from day one. Before a general becomes a general, each and every one—must pass a rigorous physical fitness test.

The words of military legends back through time echo the need for training to succeed. I love what General Douglas MacArthur said, "In no other profession are the penalties for employing untrained personnel so appalling or so irrevocable as in the military." General Matthew B. Ridgeway of the United States Army stated, "It makes no difference how fine your weapons are, or how competent your leaders; if the men in the rank are not physically hardened and highly skilled, you do not have an effective fighting force."

Wow! Talk about giving success a fighting chance! But to make an impact on a person, a community, your state, or the world, you need to make sure you're "fit" for the job in every realm, not just career intelligence.

To become the 30-second CEO, you must train to think, speak and act for success:

THINK

As a CEO, no matter what the size of your company, you must say to yourself every day: *I am what I put in my mouth, and I am what comes out of my mouth. I must operate at the highest level of integrity from my physical health, my business health, to my private life health. My life is an open book no matter how private I am. I run the company. . . .*

I have often reminded myself, *Kardashian, a pint of training will save gallons of trouble and a ton of money.* To perform at the top of my game, I need to train my body and mind constantly. And so do you. I'm not saying everything will be perfect in your work life, home life, or fitness life, but your thoughts about training your mind and body are what can set you apart from the rest.

Ask yourself: *How can I be a better provider for my home life and my corporate life?* When your genuine spirit begins to think like this, power is made available to do things you never even imagined. Things start happening, and you're able to handle life's challenges with ease.

Did you know that during exercise, the brain actually detoxifies negative, anxious, undisciplined, and self-conscious thoughts that rattle around all day? That means every time you move, you remove the toxins from your body—thanks to the brain. It's simply a must for every CEO.

SPEAK

Words have more power than you can imagine, and any CEO who allows a negative word to leave his or her lips literally gives away power. Remove negative thoughts and words from your mind and your vocabulary. Never utter a single word of negativity about yourself or your employees. Think and be positive and proactive. Here is a script I give to all my CEO clients to recite when they feel their motivation waning: *"I owe it to myself, my family, my investors (if you have them), and my employees to be in the best shape of my life. Their success, and mine, depends on it . . . I will overcome this, I am overcoming this, and I am able to handle anything that comes my way!"*

Results come from repetition. If you're not giving your body the same kind of attention you're giving your business, it shows that you're not thinking or speaking in balance. Both your body and business are organisms, not just organizations. You must flex the muscle of life in both body and business to train and enhance that life. From cognitive shape to physical shape, you must think about moving—and then move. There is just no getting around it. You must physically and mentally take care of yourself so you can effectively take care of others. Your discipline with speech and action will yield results beyond your expectations!

ACT:

In the book *Wisdom of the Generals*, author William Cohen, Ph.D., writes: "Training prepares us to face the real challenges in our profession, whatever our profession may be. Despite the fact that practically all agree that we are in the most demanding times ever, with strong competition of the highest order at the local, national and international level, many organizations spend too little time in training or don't train at all."

Why do so many companies and, presumably, CEOs consider training unnecessary? It can be expensive, take time from daily activities, require too much energy, effort, and so forth. Cohen offers advice I live by: "The best form of insurance your company can invest in is first-rate training."

Physical and mental training is essential to achieve personal and business success. To be an effective CEO you must prioritize your day and factor in time for personal development. Step out of the box and redefine what "personal development" means to you. Not all training needs to be done in a workshop, conference room, or business center. You can also energize your personal development at a gym on your exercise bike or by taking yoga three days per week for thirty minutes each session. You will earn the benefits of good health (including a strong heart), and create mental focus all at the same time.

The senior role of any executive is to clarify and communicate his or her vision. I hope this brings clarity to you so you can see the vision of a long life and a successful business opportunity!

Bring Ron Kardashian to your company!

NOTES

[1] Randy Jamison, *Florida-Times Union*.

[2] Emily Anthes, "Six Ways to Boost Brainpower," *Scientific American*, February 18, 2009. Retrieved from http://www.scientificamerican.com/article.cfm?id=six-ways-to-boost-brainpower.

[3] Daniel Amen, *Change Your Brain, Change Your Life* (Three Rivers Press, 1999).

[4] Ibid., 171.

[5] John Maxwell, Newsletter, December 2010.

[6] Alabama Coalition Against Domestic Violence, http://www.acadv.org/children.html.

[7] Ackerman, Rober and Susan Pickering, *Abused No More* (Human Services Institute, 1989).

[8] Sandra Blakeslee, "Behavior Therapy Can Change How the Brain Functions, Researchers Say," *New York Times*, September 16, 1992.

[9] Girardo & Roehl, 1978

[10] Kendall & Choudhury, 2003; Padesky, 1995.

[11] Anne-Marie R. Depape, Julie Hakim-Larson, Sylvia Voelker, Page Stewart, and Dennis L. Jackson, "Self-Talk and Emotional Intelligence in University Students," *Canadian Journal of Behavioural Science*, July 2006. Retrieval from http://www.findarticles.com/p/articles/mi_qa37171/is_200607/ai_n17180827/.

[12] Gyles Brandreth, *Your Vital Statistics: The Ultimate Book About the Average Human Being* (Lyle Stuart, 1986), 2.

[13] Gallup, http://www.gallup.com/poll/146735/Americans-Economic-Confidence-Hits-Weekly-Low-2011.aspx.

[14] Ibid.

[15] Principal Financial Group, "Concern About Financial Future Easing for Many Americans: But Retirement Savings Plans Remain Underutilized," March 8, 2011. Retrieval from www.principal.com/about/news/2011/crp-wbi-030811.htm.

[16] VOA News, "Economic Conditions Raising Stress Levels in Workers," October 11, 2010. Retrieval from http://www.voanews.com/learningenglish/home/EconomicConditions-Raising-Stress-Levels-in-Workers-104737074.html.

[17] Live Strong, http://www.livestrong.com/article/18859-health-benefits-smiling.

INDEX

About the Author

Ron Kardashian is a passionate executive life coach, a fitness authority, a national reality-television and radio personality, a published author, an educator, a dynamic conference speaker, and a NSCA-certified strength and conditioning coach.

With more than 12,000 hours of coaching under his belt, Kardashian is an influential leader who shares the stage with some of America's top advisors. Indeed, he has become a coach's coach! His work is pivotal in empowering executives to operate at high levels on every front of corporate and personal development. With his solution-based approach to big business, Kardashian has become well known as "The Solutionist." As an astute and gifted visionary Kardashian possess the secrets to helping others find the motivation and skill set to achieve any dream. If you can dream it, he can coach it.

In addition to authoring books, maintaining an active speaking schedule, and doing endorsements and private consultations, Ron is pursuing a television career with his new hit reality TV show concepts.

On the humanitarian front, Ron has established a 501 (c)3 nonprofit that is relentless in its efforts to communicate the power of bringing optimal health to all walks of life. This organization's mission is "Beautify the world through health." He does this through his worldwide educational events and collaborations with other organizations. The organization has reached more than fifty-three nations and is recognized worldwide. Ron lives in California with his wonderful wife and two children.

Booking information: Ron Kardashian is available for corporate appearances, endorsements, corporate or private coaching, speaking, autograph signings, and private appointments.

Visit him:
www.ronkardashian.com
Facebook.com/ronkardashian
Twitter.com//Ronkardashian
or E-mail: Publicity@kardashian.tv